Careers, Computers, and the Handicapped

Careers, Computers, and the Handicapped

edited by

Michael Bender
Nancy M. Pinson-Millburn
and Lee Joyce Richmond

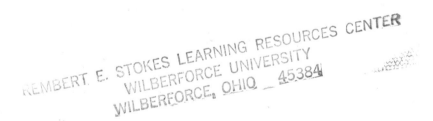

pro-ed

5341 Industrial Oaks Blvd.
Austin, Texas 78735

Library of Congress Cataloging in Publication Data
Main entry under title:

Careers, computers, and the handicapped.

Includes index.
1. Handicapped—Vocational guidance—United States—
Addresses, essays, lectures. 2. Technology—Social
aspects—United States—Addresses, essays, lectures.
I. Bender, Michael, 1943–   . I. Pinson-Millburn,
Nancy M., 1926–   . II. Richmond, Lee J., 1934–
HV1568.5.C37   1984   001.64'023'73   84-3682
ISBN 0-936104-45-7

5341 Industrial Oaks Blvd.
Austin, TX 78735

Contents

v

Contributors

Michael Bender, Ed.D.
  Director of Special Education
  John F. Kennedy Institute for
  Handicapped Children
  and
  Associate Professor of Education
  and Pediatrics
  The Johns Hopkins University and
  School of Medicine
  Baltimore, Maryland 21205

Peter P. Demyan, Ph.D.
  Assistant Professor of Education—
  Curriculum
  The Johns Hopkins University
  Baltimore, Maryland 21218

Joann Harris—Bowlsbey, Ed.D.
  Assistant Vice President
  American College Testing Program
  (ACT)
  and
  Director of the DISCOVER
  Division of ACT
  Hunt Valley, Maryland 21031

Edwin L. Herr, Ed.D
  Professor and Head
  Division of Counseling and
  Educational Psychology
  The Pennsylvania State University
  State College, Pennsylvania 16802

Charles W. Humes, Ed.D.
  Associate Professor of Counselor
  Education
  Virginia Polytechnic Institute and
  State University
  Northern Virginia Graduate Center
  Falls Church, Virginia 22042

Gail McGregor, Ed.D.
  Education Division
  The Johns Hopkins University
  Baltimore, Maryland 21218

Marion V. Panyan, Ph.D.
  Associate Professor of Education
  The Johns Hopkins University
  Baltimore, Maryland 21218

Nancy M. Pinson-Millburn, Ph.D.
  Formerly, Program Director
  Center of Rehabilitation and
  Manpower Services
  University of Maryland 20742
  and
  Coordinator of Research, Vocational
  Guidance, and Career Development
  Maryland State Department of
  Education
  Baltimore, Maryland 21201

Donald R. Rabush, Ed.D.
  Associate Professor of Special
  Education
  Western Maryland College
  Westminster, Maryland 21157

Lee Joyce Richmond, Ph.D.
  Professor of Counseling
  and Human Development
  the Johns Hopkins University
  Baltimore, Maryland 21218

Lynn Rogers, M.A.
  Counseling and Human
  Development
  The Johns Hopkins University
  Baltimore Maryland 21218

Gilbert B. Schiffman, O.D., Ed.D.
  Professor and Education
  Coordinator
  Programs for Exceptional Children
  The Johns Hopkins University
  Baltimore, Maryland 21218

Donald E. Super, Ph.D.
  Adjunct Professor of Psychology
  and Education
  University of Florida
  Gainesville, Florida 32611
  and Professor Emeritus of
  Psychology and Education
  International Coordinator of the
  Work Importance Study
  Teachers College
  Columbia University
  New York, New York 10027

Preface

This text provides concerned educators, counselors, scientists, administrators, and policy makers with persuasive evidence that technology can and will play a vitally important role in the career development and vocational maturity of the handicapped youth and adult population. It is intended to provoke the consideration of new ways in which the helping professions can work with their colleagues in the hard sciences on behalf of these individuals. In a real sense, this book celebrates the potential merger of a liberating vision with available technology—an often elusive educational goal whose realization has particular significance for the unserved and underserved disabled in our society.

The principal genesis of this collaborative effort by 13 writers of considerable expertise was a spirited colloquium on the campus of Johns Hopkins University in May of 1982. As the conceptualizer for that event, the Education Division of the University's School of Continuing Studies was taking the logical next step in the kind of transdisciplinary venture for which it has become recognized: one emphasizing field applications of inquiry and research findings across diverse academic fields. In this instance, one of several stimuli was the 1981 Report of the Johns Hopkins First National Search for the Application of Personal Computing to Aid the Handicapped; a year-long study that resulted in the selection of 97 winning submissions from a national application of over one thousand. Still another impetus driving the conference managers was the recognition that—good intentions to the contrary—devastating statistics of unemployment and other, less quantifiable, indices of personal and social isolation continued to be associated with far too many of this nation's handicapped.

Given this enormous challenge in the form of an intensive 2-day agenda, participant writers came prepared to synthesize their varied experiences and ideologies before the most astute of audiences: the handicapped, their employers, and key members of the university community. Not only did these professional leaders probe deeply into the implications of the computer age for the disabled, the unfolding agenda required them to grapple with still other issues of importance to both the provider and the consumer of rehabilitation and counseling services.

Among these were related implications for the future training and retraining of the helping practitioner, distinctions between the congenitally, adventitiously, and socially handicapped in terms of their passage through traditional stages of career development, vocational skill training for the impaired or impeded, the circumvention of handicap through the application of simple to complex technologies, the democratization of the computer for the learning disabled and sensorially deprived, and the laying to rest of certain myths and fears associated with the union of the human organism and the prostheses afforded by technology.

Much more than the results of that dialogue is explicated in this volume. To the degree and extent possible, prepared and extemporaneous insights are joined in the chapters that follow. It is clear that not all of these writers agree. Their terminology, their proposed methodologies, and even their personal philosophies about the handicapped differ and, occasionally, conflict sharply. Some authors speak from a counseling perspective, others from either a rehabilitation, educational, or vocational base. Specialists caution generalists, and not all are as comfortable as others in venturing into the field of computers and related technologies. In the view of the editors, these distinctions add weight and meaning to their commentary. Their work combines to serve as a research and action agenda that is compelling in both its magnitude and practicality, urgent in its call for the most creative of society's alliances and inventions to be deployed for its less advantaged members.

Introduction

Nancy M. Pinson-Millburn

In a statistical sense, exceptional people are those whose learning and/or adaptive characteristics place them at either end of the so-called normal curve. On the one hand, they could be described as gifted; on the other, as cognitively, socially, or physiologically handicapped. Both are special populations in need of special attention. Within this text, we are looking at that individual whose disability has resulted in a reduction or loss of function that inhibits or handicaps full social, educational, or vocational participation. Habilitation or rehabilitation is indicated as primary mediation to be employed by skilled professionals.

Distinguishing this volume from others written on the subject is its incorporation of an entirely new thesis: the union of computer technology with human mediation systems on behalf of this population. This union, now in its infancy, holds the potential and the promise for dramatically improving the quality of life for more than 25 million of our citizens at a fraction of the social costs incurred through the application of custodial or institutional remedies.

THE TEXT: A BRIEF SYNOPSIS

Chapter 1, written by Peter Demyan and Gilbert Schiffman, points out the discrepancies between a legal and moral mandate to serve the handicapped and the actual identification and allocation of available resources to achieve that goal. The authors argue for computer literacy of educators and counselors as forcefully as they present the human challenge to technicians, engineers, and computer programmers. These writers see the microcomputer as not only a communication tool for the individual student but as an invaluable aid to curriculum development, instruction, and program management for these youths.

Chapter 2, written by Michael Bender, addresses the hard issues associated with vocational training of handicapped youths and adults. Bender cites evidence that our social and educational institutions have not kept pace with available technologies and tools that can facilitate the vocational maturity of this group. He points out that opportunities for the handicapped to become self-sustaining members of society through the provision of skill training continue to be limited in quality and accessibility. Bender notes that traditional methods of training the disabled, such as sheltered workshops, work activities centers, and adult activity centers—although well-intentioned—perpetuate the notion of piecework or caretaking as sufficient. Although educational institutions offering skill training are attempting to mainstream the more insistent handicapped petitioner, vocational educators admit to a lack of understanding experience in making the necessary modifications to the training setting. Bender cites the community-based training model as having the greatest promise in bridging traditional and future-oriented strategies of integrating handicapped workers into the workplace and offers a convincing argument for its success.

Chapter 3, written by Donald Super, first establishes important distinctions between those groups with either acquired or congenital handicaps in order to present his thesis. He points out the dangers of applying any single theory to this group, and offers the possibility that several in combination can be usefully employed. In discussing the discontinuity of development that characterizes most handicapped individuals, Super underscores the value of compensatory structures. These are similar in content to those interventions applied by professionals who work with those whose careers are multiple-trial or unstable in nature. He further notes that the developmental tasks of childhood, adolescence, and adulthood need not be viewed as rigid or fixed in order or intensity, but when applied to the handicapped should be seen as guidelines for transitions between stages. Super concludes his thoughtful treatment with the observation that the challenge of career development for the disabled lies in communication, whether visual, motor, auditory, or spoken. It is a challenge that he believes can be met by resourceful practitioners.

Chapter 4, written by Marion Panyon and Gail McGregor, provides a dual perspective on the strengths and the limitations of the national thrust in career education as it relates to the education of the handicapped. They observe that although its comprehensiveness is one of its greatest attractions, career education is too often confused with vocational education or vocational rehabilitation and thus linked with a goal of gainful employment for those involved. According to Panyon and McGregor, this linkage has resulted in the assumption that only higher functioning individuals can be candidates, thus removing access by the more severely disabled to those pretraining experiences defined as career awareness, career orientation, and actual job skill development. They suggest that a totally functional career education curriculum for the handicapped would succeed where academic or vocational curricula alone cannot. Panyon and McGregor provide a scenario in which life skills, social skills, and vocational skills are learned and continuously measured using microtechnologies, support systems, behavior management, and individualized instruction.

Chapter 5, written by Donald Rabush, speaks of the physically handicapped as a population far larger than the public's equation of it with the motor impaired. He reminds us that sensory impairments (speech, vision, hearing) and health impairments (cerebral palsy, epilepsy, cardiac disorders) are also included under this rubric. This being the case, Rabush notes that career development needs vary as much among these groups as they do across the population as a whole. He also observes that, while special education may have resulted in "equal" education for those mainstreamed by legislative fiat, an unequal situation has been created in fulfilling the career expectations of the disabled. Rabush believes this is due to the limited training of professional educators in areas other than the cognitive or academic aspects of special education. A further compounding factor is the scarcity of materials and tools designed expressly for the handicapped person's exposure to and exploration of the career applications of his or her own interests. He proposes that acceptance of the disabled by teachers and employers must begin by publicizing the exceptional gains made by extraordinary people—people such as employers who have redesigned or created new job environments for the disabled and have also seen new records set in production and attendance, teachers who have developed their own software curriculum for handicapped students, and the handicapped themselves who return to schools and earlier employers as role models and advisors.

Chapter 6, written by Joann Harris-Bowlsbey, is a cogent argument for the computer as a motivating agent specifically with the young who embrace technology without anxiety and with those handicapped individuals who view the computer as a nonjudgmental and patient ally in performing a specific task. As creator of two computerized interactive guidance systems, Harris-Bowlsbey is persuasive in her knowledge and enthusiasm, particularly in the specifics provided on the multiple-role capacity of the computer. (She notes that if computers and counselors are doing the same things in career guidance, something is very much out of line!) Harris-Bowlsbey follows her comprehensive discussion of the computer as facilitator to career and life planning by making two points. First, she reemphasizes the value of the well-programmed computer to the handicapped by sampling a wide range of career environments and work requirements in nonpunitive ways. Second, by providing recent research data on the effectiveness of the counselor and computer in combination, she makes a strong plea for professional acceptance of and affection for what is to many still strange and unapproachable.

Chapter 7, coauthored by Charles W. Humes and Lee Richmond, extends the Harris-Bowlsbey premise into additional realms of career information and delivery for specifically handicapped groups. Although their focus is on computer-assisted systems, other potential modes of prosthesis for the disabled are suggested. Humes and Richmond develop a broad view of technological assistance as it might apply not only to concerns of schooling, but to interpersonal relationships, work adjustment, transportation, personal image building, and other challenges common to the handicapped and their more advantaged peers. In developing their chapter, the authors called upon recent advances in these macro- and microsystems by tapping current research as well as the initiatives undertaken by lead agencies in the public and private sectors.

Chapter 8, written by Edwin Herr, addresses the problems and the challenges of training those who will work with the handicapped in career development delivery skills. Herr's review of the counseling and rehabilitation literature spans a 15-year period in which only a handful of articles addressing such training could be located. Herr then synthesizes those few citations and offers his interpretation of the majority's silence: The counselor-generalist is trained to view *all* people as "exceptional" and therein lies the problem. Even those trained in the exceptionalities, he notes, such as rehabilitation counselors, school psychologists, or special educators, prefer to write about or conduct research in areas other than career development. Herr's search of the in-service or practitioner workshop literature is more rewarding. Here, he finds direct experience with numerous examples of training in attitude change, simulating the handicapping condition over a period of time and external stresses, and other instances in which understanding was substituted for ignorance or avoidance. Herr sees the professional practitioner far in advance of the student in training because of the forced exposure to the law and social pressures: subjects rarely discussed in the traditional counselor education program.

The Conclusion, written by Nancy Pinson-Millburn, draws the text together through review, synthesis, and considered recommendations for action. These recommendations are offered as implications for research and for policy, and will receive further input from two groups: our allies in the hard sciences upon whom we will continue to rely, and representatives of the disabled and handicapped community who will grade us on the veracity and feasibility of those recommendations.

Following the text is "the Resource Guide to Computer Technology and the Handicapped," which represents the careful investigation by Lynn

Rogers of The Johns Hopkins Graduate School into a representative sample of resources found in refereed publications associated with a wide range of professional groups. Additionally, Rogers supplements these annotations with listings of the more prominent journals in the fields under consideration. Other resources cited have tapped several bases such as ABLE DATA, NARIC, and the SOFTWARE Clearinghouse.

Acknowledgments

This book is the result of the Hodson Trust Colloquium, *Future Perspectives and Realities: Career Development for Exceptional People*, which was sponsored by the Johns Hopkins University School of Continuing Studies. We would like to acknowledge numerous individuals for their information and insightful comments during the Conference. These include: Mr. Paul Hazen of the Johns Hopkins Applied Physics Laboratory; Dr. Leonard Hasman, Research Specialist of the National Center for Research in Vocational Education of the Ohio State University; Mr. E. Neil Carey, Senior Staff Specialist, Career and Community Based Education, Maryland State Department of Education; and Dr. Peter Valletutti, Professor and Department Head of Special Education, Coppin State College.

We also would like to acknowledge those individuals who participated in the conference and represented employment and consumer perspectives. These include: Robert Grohol, Senior Vice President of the Beneficial Management Corporation; Sally Greene, Supervisor of Special Recruiting for the Chesapeake and Potomac Telephone Company; Michelle Lavin, District Handicapped Program Manager; Internal Revenue Service; David Thompson, 504 Legislation Coordinator of the Maryland State Department of Education; and Ruth C. Brown-Pear, Specialist in Special Programs (Handicapped and Disadvantaged), Maryland State Department of Education, Division of Vocational and Technical Education.

The Editors would also like to thank Ruth Lisansky, Counselor-Coordinator of Career Services, Towson State University, who coordinated the arrangements for the conference with the assistance of Connie Harris and Lenore Lynch, Johns Hopkins University doctoral students.

A special acknowledgment is offered to Dr. Roman Verhallen, former Dean of the Evening College, and Dr. Stanley Gabor, Dean of the Johns Hopkins School of Continuing Studies, for their support in the development and the continuation of the ideals established by this colloquium.

The Editors also wish to acknowledge Mr. Zanvyl Krieger for his support in providing funds for the development of this book and his continual support for projects involving the handicapped.

Lastly, a special acknowledgment is offered to Diane Levy, CMT, for her typing and retyping of the manuscript.

Computers and Exceptional Persons

Peter P. Demyan and Gilbert B. Schiffman

RELATIONSHIPS BETWEEN COMPUTERS AND EXCEPTIONAL PERSONS

> Initial exploration of microcomputer use has already touched every exceptionality. The technology is here but the application is still in its infancy. Much is still experimental; much requires an abundance of equipment and is extremely expensive . . . In time it is expected that much of the equipment will cost no more and be no larger than a pocket calculator. In the meantime, the knowledge of what has been developed and the creative imagination special educators have used so far should be the catalyst for change in the immediate future.
>
> Taber (1983)

> In general, there has been a paucity of research that has specifically attempted to assess the effectiveness of different technologies or their employment as alternatives to other approaches. Many of the conclusions that have been drawn concerning the application of technology to the education of the handicapped have been based on logic more than empirical data.
>
> Blackhurst and Hofmeister (1980)

The topic of the exceptionalities in educational environments is not new. Indeed, Dexter (1977) traced the written records in the field to the 1500s. Other works (Doll, 1962; Kirk & Johnson, 1951) have chronicled special education services since the early 19th century. Dunn (1973), with others, placed the field's watershed in the early 1950s. Van Osdol and Shane (1977) highlighted the key legislative actions that supported direct service activities, culminating in Public Law 94–142. In this chapter, the

1950s shall serve as the beginning date for substantive programmatic emphasis on the exceptional person.

Similarly, the computer and its role in education can be seen as "not new." In more primitive forms, the use of programmed instruction and computer-assisted instruction can also be traced to the early 1950s (Taylor, 1980). A resourceful individual can trace the underpinnings of the computer to the time of the Pascaline machines of the 1640s (Evans, 1980). The first major peak of interest in the field of computer technology came about in the early to mid-1960s (Bunderson & Faust, 1976) as did programmed instruction. In this chapter, the modern use of the computer in instruction is set in the early 1960s.

What is remarkable about both areas (computers and exceptionalities) is the explosive growth in interest and knowledge in each since their beginnings; and it seems that such a growth pattern will continue into the future. Dunn (1973), for example, originally cited such factors forcing "rethinking" in the exceptionalities as: (1) social changes; (2) management processes; (3) recategorizing; (4) mainstreaming; (5) fiscal restraints; (6) interprofessional group blendings; (7) altered teacher preparation practices; (8) rise in numbers of the multiply disabled; (9) behavioral objectives/modification movements; (10) increases in pre-high/high/post-high school programs; (11) more and better research; and (12) inclusion of the gifted.

Evans (1980) singled out several factors that will induce reconceptualizations in many fields due to improvements in computers: (1) the demise of money; (2) the death of the printed word; (3) the decline of the knowledge professions (teaching, medicine, and law); and (4) a rise in ultraintelligent machines. Evans also emphasized the rapid growth of the power and efficiency of the computer through an analogy to the development of the automobile, which, if it had progressed as rapidly, would be of Rolls Royce quality, cost $3, deliver 3 million miles to the gallon, and possess the power needed to drive the Queen Elizabeth II. The point is this: any discussion of the two areas—computers and the exceptionalities—needs to include a caveat similar to that applicable at the level of subatomics, where the Heisenberg Uncertainty Principle applies. With fast-moving particles, one can assess either momentum or mass, not both. Similarly, one can fix a view of the status of either computers or exceptionalities, but by the time that is done, the other has moved on.

In sum, a broader tapestry (which includes at least three threads) must be the context of the present discussion: (1) the backdrop of social, economic, and educational upheavals in the present society (Naisbitt, 1982); (2) the virtually daily revision of the limits, potentials, and functions of the computer and related technologies; and (3) the redefinition and reconceptualization of the exceptionalities as normal/exceptional boundaries blur (L'Abate & Curtis, 1975).

In this chapter, a case is made for the rethinking of some categories of the exceptionalities. It is not done for the sake of adding to the mix of definitions, category systems, or theoretical arguments, but to reflect what constitutes functional examples of such new niches given the computer/exceptionality interface. Five such categories are presented: (1) the physically/mentally/emotionally exceptional child; (2) the physically/mentally/emotionally exceptional adult; (3) the educationally exceptional youth; (4) the academically exceptional child/youth/adult; and (5) the socially/vocationally exceptional youth/adult. The common thread through all five groups is the computer and its related technologies. In no case, however, does the high technology aspect stand alone. There is a companion focus on what Naisbitt (1982) has identified as "high touch" or personal. That high tech/high touch mix will be seen as a catalyst and conduit for reaching, supplementing, and elevating the exceptional person.

Finally, the closing argument in the chapter underscores the need for a broader and more comprehensive view of education and its role in our social structure. The case is also made for a need to understand better the processes of curriculum development, program evaluation, and instructional processes as increasingly diverse groups become involved in the education of exceptional persons in high tech/high touch environments.

The chapter proceeds as follows: first, a conceptual overview is developed; next, instances in practice of each of the five exceptionalities categories and computer technology are presented; and, finally, the educational imperative is addressed.

AN EVER-CHANGING TAPESTRY

As planners and groups scramble for plans for the year 2000, time must be taken to look more closely at social changes. First, the computer is being introduced at all levels. From the microprocessors in automobiles, microwave ovens, wristwatches, industrial devices, and computers/calculators to the fields of education, medicine, art, music, and the world of work, vast changes are already in place and more are on the way (Evans, 1979; Naisbitt, 1982; Taylor, 1980). Naisbitt (1982) "summed up" American history in three words: "farmer, laborer, clerk." Tied with the rapid advances in the computer are advances in communication as both IBM and AT&T begin to merge into one functional system of information flow, storage, and access. Third, the rapid shifting of economic reality to that of partnerships among former adversaries

(Galbraith, 1983)—labor, business/industry, and government—in the form of multinational alliances and corporations is quickly becoming status quo.

It is somewhat ironic that projection for the year 2000 is less a gamble than projection for the year 1990 (Evans, 1980). Perhaps because, by the time 2000 rolls around, most projections will have been abandoned.

The relationships between this rapid social/technological/economic change and computers and the exceptional person can now be addressed. What is a barrier to either field today will not likely be so in the very near future. With the rapid deployment of the microcomputer and related larger systems, problems of adaptive devices, programs, and systems, once prohibitive—both economically and technically—are no longer so. Both software and hardware can be custom developed to meet the needs of the exceptional user as imbedded (in-the-body) devices are refined (Evans, 1980). The program examples given later in this chapter relied on adapted and/or modified systems.

Finally, the services to handicapped people and their contributions to the same society both demand reconceptualization. Computers can be used by many severely physically disabled individuals who have any reasonably consistent muscle action enabling them—sometimes for the first time in their lives—to communicate through microcomputers and voice systems. Social and private agencies (departments of occupational training, corporations, university personnel) are becoming involved with persons formerly ignored or relegated to inappropriate traditional school settings to make them competitive with their more able peers and, in some cases (such as entry-level computer programming), to excel beyond them.

The excitement and the challenge of the future is vested in the understanding that none of these changes is likely to be lessened in the near future. The threat exists, however, that old methods, old alliances, old patterns, and old thinking will still be used. Those who confidently make predictions for the year 2000 and plan for it accordingly adhere to a future image that has lost its viability—the straight-line projection of *a* singular future (Shane, 1971, 1973; Shane & Tabler, 1981). Rather, there is a multiplicity of alterable, possible futures whose ultimate emergence depends more on held values and actions (or lack thereof) than limitations in technology and science.

A RETHINKING OF EXCEPTIONALITIES CATEGORIES

As the notion that schooling is *identical* in concept to education loses practical significance in modern society, so will the credibility of access to employment through singular, uniform, and traditional avenues of preparation. If the continuum of education is seen as lifelong, from cradle to grave, then a rapidly changing technology has meaning throughout a person's lifetime educational growth. Coupling the broadening of educational services and agencies to the advances in high technology has had a major impact on exceptional persons.

This impact is notable on several levels. These include: accessment of the exceptional person, academic and interpersonal training, and vocational/career skills training.

Figure 1.1 presents the interface between the computer and related technologies and the exceptional person. The dual-headed arrows indicate interaction between computer and persons. The category boxes show the relative age classifications *increase* from infant through adult.

With the exclusion of the academically and educationally exceptional categories, the conditions of exceptionality depicted in Figure 1.1 have multiple sources. However, in practice, the academic and educational categories also rest on physical, mental, and emotional bases (psychomotor, cognitive, and affective) as well as social bases (Derr, 1973). Common to all category areas are the aspects of accessment, vocational, career, and life concerns.

The physically/mentally/emotionally and the academically exceptional categories are conventionally defined. The subpopulations are chosen to illustrate the programs discussed below. The remaining category areas are newly constructed for this chapter.

The most conventional of the three is that of the physically/mentally/emotionally exceptional adult/youth. This is the group commonly assigned to vocational rehabilitation. They may have a visible or nonapparent disability. The problems range from (in the project cited) weakness of the digital extremities to quadriplegia to manic-depressiveness to cerebral palsy. The goal is to make the individual employable.

The second group is that which has been labeled juvenile delinquents, dropouts, educationally disabled, or, most recently, disadvantaged. They are the educationally exceptional. Their problems range from lack of basic academic skills to social interaction deficiencies to vocational ill-preparedness. The goal is to provide these youths and young adults with a better chance for success through placement in service (military, civil, and social), gainful employment, academic reinstatement, or academic/program advancement.

The final group is the one that has most recently emerged—the socially and vocationally exceptional. This population has been called the displaced worker, the technologically unemployed, or the phased-out worker group. They are generally victims of a changing work and economic environment that makes their skills functionally and voca-

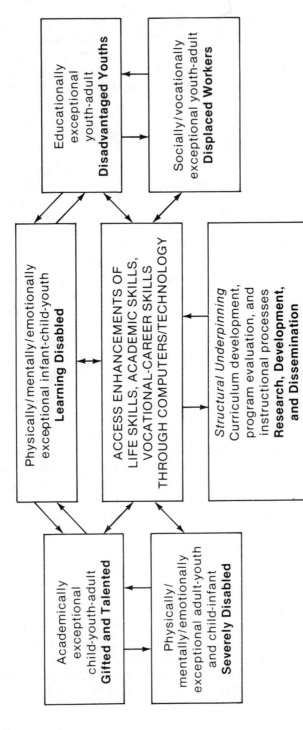

Figure 1.1. A relationships diagram among the elements of the computer-exceptional interface and the five selected areas of exceptionalities.

tionally obsolete. They are technology's "push-outs." The programs for this group (as with the disadvantaged youths, for example) are best implemented in an interagency context within an individualized, adaptive framework. This element of the exceptional population groupings is likely to show the most phenomenal growth in the near future as high technologies (e.g., robotics, computer-managed assembly, and computer-aided drafting) come "on line" in business and industry (Evans, 1980; Naisbitt, 1982).

The condition that underlies the exceptionality in the three areas of the physically/mentally/emotionally exceptional (both types) and the academically exceptional are likely to be lifelong. The other two areas—educationally and socially/vocationally exceptional—are more prone to remediation (at least temporarily effective) or removal of the exceptional condition.

Educationally Exceptional Youth and Adult: The Disadvantaged

In a report issued by the House Subcommittee on elementary, secondary, and vocational education (Perkins, 1977), it was pointed out that since 1967 (to 1977) the dropout rate for whites was constant at 11% and the nonwhite rate was declining and approaching that figure. Their hypothesis was that:

> . . . there is a body of students, perhaps around 10 or 11 percent, who are not cut out in terms of their aptitudes and ability for the kinds of implicit goals, and functions, of the school system. Consequently, *attempts to directly reduce dropout rates may themselves not be in the public interest and not in the interest of the dropout students. Alternative forms of education may be appropriate.* (pp. 568–569) (italics added). . . . This question becomes increasingly pressing when one sees the *movement toward an information society* making credentials as well as the ability to work with written symbols a key part of our society and its upward economic mobility. *To force all into that mold may be as serious an error as to fail those who are able.* (p. 569) (italics added).

Physically/Mentally/Emotionally Exceptional Adult/Youth: The Severely Disabled

A few years ago, a teacher of special needs youths was stricken with a paralysis that made it impossible for her to speak or to sit at a greater than 45-degree angle. With one side of her body and her voice paralyzed, she is now using a portable microcomputer and speech synthesizer to communicate. In addition, she is enrolled in a program to become an entry-level computer programmer. A few years ago, this was unthinkable; a few months ago, just impossible; and today, a reality. Such is the potency of the computer for aiding the severely disabled to be productive once again, and (as the following underscores) on a competitive basis with their more able-bodied peers.

Beginning in 1973, the IBM corporation, in conjunction with state and local agencies, helped to found and coordinate a network of rehabilitation programs in data processing on the national level. Some 25 such sites are currently approved members of the Association of Rehabilitation Programs in Data Processing (ARPDP), and a half-dozen others are pending. The programs have four basic components (ARPDP, 1981):

> *Clients* who can be trained to meet the employability standards of local businesses, *Jobs* which occur in the area served by the project, a *Means for Training* the clients to perform the needed operations, and a *Business Advisory Council* made up of local data processing professionals. If even one of these components is not available, it is unlikely that the program will succeed. (p. 1-1).

Socially/Vocationally Exceptional Youth/Adult: The Displaced Worker

These terms are all too familiar to those who have worked with the exceptionalities. First, there is the belief that the condition does not really exist—it must be something else. Second comes the denial that it will be permanent—it will go away. Finally comes acceptance and searching—ideally—for alternatives. This scenario also describes the displaced worker. Like the severely disabled (the recently paralyzed, for example) they have tried denying, waiting, and, finally, accepting and searching. Traditionally, they have come up dry. As one unemployed steelworker put it: "You are caught in a no-win situation. You cannot get other than minimum wage and temporary jobs because employers believe that as soon as the steel mill calls, you'll leave. And you would, too, but they are never going to call you any more."

CONCLUSION

In many instances, the learnings and personal resources in one area are transferable to another. The very nature of high technology demands this. However, if arbitrary conventions, definitions, conceptual "turfs," and the like are allowed to continue, many of the learnings and advances in one area will be obtained without the networking so readily available if all aspects of exceptionalities were to be considered.

With its universal application in all our lives, the computer may be able to do what educational and school-based programs have never been able to do—accommodate the true needs of the handicapped client, not for efficiency, but for effectiveness.

In theory, most individuals recognize the difference between schooling and education. In practice, for many of the exceptionalities, schooling (and all the history, structure, values, and processes—good or bad—that accompany it) is the conceptual structure for delivery of instructional services in many areas. Mainstreaming, while an honest attempt to address this issue for handicapped persons, continually fights an uphill battle to be effective. Furthermore, mainstreaming tends to break down once one leaves the narrow confines of the school environment (elementary, secondary, or postsecondary) and enters the multiagency reality of the general culture.

As the numbers of individual agencies coming into contact with the exceptional person increase, more than simply multiplying resources is indicated. A change *in kind*, not just degree, is needed. Hence, curriculum development must address multiple agency points of view, adopt workable decision strategies that cut across agency and/or organizational boundaries, and be responsive to the complex constellation of demands in the "real world."

Professionals in the fields of the exceptionalities have a head start on adaptation to that real world through having had to deal with it for decades—sometimes pleading, sometimes demanding, sometimes fighting—but always dealing. Now, those who are not in the habit of such complex needs management are asking for assistance with new "special" populations. Those agencies that formerly viewed the plight of the exceptional person as "someone else's" problem have begun to take a long look at themselves and have come to realize that, without cooperative efforts, "We have met the enemy, and he is us" (as the comic character Pogo so aptly observed).

Finally, the practices of program evaluation must be modernized. No longer can the passing "summative evaluation" of a program—no matter how data-thick—be allowed to suffice. A high touch human approach that actively incorporates both quantitative and qualitative measures must be developed along with the emergent programs for the exceptionalities. This human sciences approach will demand naturalistic as well as scientific (Guba & Lincoln, 1981) methods. In addition, attention must be given to quality control and follow-up evaluations. Too many "one-year" or "until-the-funding-stopped" wonders dot the programmatic history of the field. Program developers must learn, in the final analysis, to *do a few things well and do them completely*.

The relationship between the computer and exceptional persons in the near future will not only be interactive, but soon reciprocal. The only limitation to such productive relationships between exceptional people and computer technology will be the speed with which these relationships are embraced and fostered by society.

REFERENCES

ARPDP. (1981). *Computer programming training for severely disabled persons*. (FCA #26P-60319/3-08). Washington, DC: Rehabilitation Services Administration of the Department of Education, January.
Blackhurst, A. E., & Hofmeister, A. M. (1980). Technology in special education. In L. Mann and D. A. Sabatino (Eds.), *The fourth review of special education*. New York: Grune & Stratton.
Bunderson, C. V., & Faust, G. W. (1976). Programmed and computer assisted instruction. In N. L. Gage (Ed.), *The psychology of teaching methods* (The seventy-fifth yearbook of the National Society for the Study of Education, part I). Chicago: University of Chicago Press.
Derr, R. L. (1973). *A taxonomy of social purposes of public schools*. New York: David McKay.
Dexter, B. L. (1977). *Special Education and the classroom teacher*. Springfield, IL: Charles C Thomas.
Doll, E. E. (1962). A historical survey of research and management of mental retardation in the United States. In P. E. Trapp and P. Himelstein (Eds.), *Readings on the exceptional child*. New York: Appleton-Century-Crofts.
Dunn, L. M. (Ed.). (1973). *Exceptional children in the schools* (2nd ed.). New York: Holt, Rinehart & Winston.
Evans, C. (1980). *The micro millennium*. New York: Viking.
Galbraith, W. K. (1983). The American economy in an age of sadness. First annual Elizabeth Morrissy Endowed Lecture held at College of Notre Dame, Baltimore, March 15.
Kirk, S., & Johnson, G. O. (1951). *Educating the retarded child*. Boston: Houghton Mifflin.
L'Abate, L., & Curtis, L. T. (1975). *Teaching the exceptional child*. Philadelphia: Saunders.
Naisbitt, J. (1982). *Megatrends*. New York: Warner Books.
Perkins, C. D. (1977). *Part I: General issues in elementary and secondary education*. Hearings held on May 10, 11, 1977. Washington, DC: U.S. Government Printing Office.
Shane, H. G. (1971). Future-planning as a means of shaping eduational change. In R. M. McClure (Ed.), *The curriculum: Retrospect and prospect* (The seventieth yearbook of the National Society for the Study of Education, part I). Chicago: University of Chicago Press.
Shane, H. G. (1973). *The educational significance of the future*. Bloomfield, In: Phi Delta Kappa.
Shane, H. G., & Tabler, M. B. (1981). *Education for a new millennium*. Bloomfield, IN: Phi Delta Kappa.

Taber, F. M. (1983). *Microcomputers in special education*. Reston, VA: The Council for Exceptional Children.

Taylor, R. P. (Ed.). (1980). *The computer in the school: Tutor, tool, tutee*. New York: Teachers College Press.

Van Osdol, W. R., & Shane, D. G. (1977). *An introduction to exceptional children* (2nd ed.). Dubuque, IA. Wm. C. Brown.

2

Vocational Training for the Handicapped

Michael Bender

The history of successful vocational training for individuals who deviate from the general population in physical appearance, intellectual ability, and adaptive behavior is discouraging. Historically, society has ignored attempts to provide training for the handicapped for several reasons. Among these are: (1) prevailing economic conditions; (2) existing attitudes; (3) lack of adequate educational and medical knowledge; and (4) confusion over what legally constitutes a disability.

It is important to realize that the greatest impediment to training the handicapped today is not our lack of technological knowledge, but our lack of a cohesive and integrated approach to coordinating existing resources in the domains of vocational assessment, training, placement, and follow-up.

There is sufficient evidence to suggest that we can be successful in training the handicapped of all functioning levels. Curricula exist (Bender & Valletutti, 1976, 1981) that demonstrate that the handicapped can indeed improve in such domains as self-help, communication, socialization, and motor skills, and in those areas associated with functional academics. Many of these individuals go on to have successful experiences at work and in community settings. Unfortunately, the vast majority of handicapped individuals, and especially older mentally retarded persons, are still taught within the framework of inappropriate curricula, treated with benevolent and malevolent attitudes, and trained with inadequate and inappropriate vocational programming methodology. Furthermore, career education is constantly confused with vocational education, adding to the overall programming dilemma. Similarly, the use of the term *handicapped* is often limited to one's expertise or familiarity with a special type of client population.

Historically, attention to vocational programs for the handicapped is believed to have begun in 1784 when Valentine Haui established the first training school and workshop for the blind in Paris (Hansen & Haring, 1980). Unfortunately, not much has changed since then. The first workshops tended to address the needs of those with sensory impairments, especially the blind; this evolved into workshops being developed for indigent and poor populations. It was not until after the Industrial Revolution that interest in vocational training changed its focus. At this time, vocational programming, usually known as rehabilitation programming, was predominantly designed for victims of industrial accidents.

World War I and returning disabled veterans created the need for more rehabilitative efforts. It was not, however, until the Rehabilitation Act of 1973 that the severely handicapped population was finally recognized as a societal group needing vocational training. Gradually, the term *habilitation* replaced the term *rehabilitation* because most severely handicapped individuals did not require retraining but initial training. This fact was especially true for mentally retarded individuals who could not return to a skill level they had never initially achieved.

Before addressing the imperative issue of vocational and career training for handicapped individuals, it is important first to view the merits of providing such services on the basis of the objectives it presumes to achieve. First, vocational training programs allow an individual to be self-sufficient based on the concept that work is good. Second, they tend to enhance an individual's self-concept and feeling of worth. Third, they also provide a healthy and valued social outlet for individuals who normally would be sheltered from contact with their peers or with other members of society.

The 1970s resulted in a significant growth of federal programs and a general support by society for vocational education and rehabilitation programs. It was also during this time that vocational training methodology and approaches increased in number and in kind.

Vocational training programs for the handicapped have traditionally been delivered in three types of settings (Hansen & Haring, 1980). First, *sheltered workshops* represented a controlled environment and have historically been the place where severely handicapped individuals work. Sheltered workshops are traditionally nonprofit rehabilitation or habilitation facilities that utilize contracts and piecework renumeration systems. Second, *work activity centers* were often a component of sheltered workshops and have typically been used to serve those handicapped individuals who are so severely disabled that the number of products they produce is minimal. Third, *adult activity centers* were established for individuals with training needs in the most fundamental processes. Included are the teaching of toileting, eating, ambulation, communication, and all of those related skills associated with the daily living and self-care areas (Hansen & Haring, 1980; Lynch 1979).

Today, the emphasis is shifting to *community-based training programs*. These specific programs provide job training skills on an actual job site, thereby providing realism in the training effort. In many instances, community-based training programs have integrated nonhandicapped and handicapped co-workers in joint ventures. These programs not only prepare clients for new work environments, but also, when appropriate, modify the work environment for their special needs. Most community-based training programs are habilitative in nature and not rehabilitative because they are often the first work experience for severely handicapped individuals in the community.

The treatment of the handicapped in terms of providing comprehensive vocational training programs has been minimal. Significant advances in society's treatment of the handicapped in the vocational area did not occur until the 19th century when there was an increase in the development of rehabilitation programs. Most notable were the programs that were implemented for blind and deaf populations. These programs were followed by services for the mentally retarded and medically based restoration programs for the mentally ill and physically disabled. It has not been until the past decade that the educational needs of the handicapped have included vocational and career goals. With this acknowledgment has come the realization that successful training efforts for a population of individuals with severe handicaps ultimately may result in possible employment and careers, thus freeing some handicapped individuals from total reliance on society.

Professionals from the fields of guidance, psychology, special education, medicine, and disciplines related to therapeutic interventions have struggled to develop programs for these individuals. Unfortunately, and ironically, almost all of these disciplines have worked in isolation. This isolation is the real problem we face in the 20th century, an isolation that results in information being taught in one area and opposite and conflicting information being presented in another.

BEHAVIOR TRAINING AND MANAGEMENT

Over the past three decades, vocational research has shifted from studying different motivational or behavioral management strategies to investigating the skills and training techniques that are useful in the rehabilitative process. Studies such as those by Crosson (1969), which showed the necessity of instructional cues to train the severely mentally retarded individual, Bender (1978), which showed the advantages of using imitative training to teach the mentally retarded, and Gold (1972), which provided research on the utilization of the task analysis approach for the mentally retarded, ushered in a new philosophical base on how to teach vocational skills to the handicapped. Equally important has been the realization that although skill acquisition is important, training in the behavioral and interpersonal domains is also critical.

Over the last three decades in the United States, there has been a noticeable shift from the vocational research areas that were initiated during the early 1950s and 1960s. These eras were characterized by great emphasis on motivational and behavioral management strategies for improving vocational programming. A decade later, studies tended to indicate that the emphasis had shifted, with more attention on productivity and how it can be altered by manipulating various components of the vocational process. These include: (1) manipulation of consequences, including changing goals; (2) offering handicapped workers encouragement; (3) offering them interval and piecework pay; (4) social contingencies; and (5) the development of token economies.

A behavioral training approach to vocational training involves different behavior-environment interactions; that is, there are certain factors of training that one must know. For example, one must understand the antecedent cue that immediately precedes a behavior as well as the behavior itself. Additionally, one must also know the events that immediately follow the behavior (i.e., the consequences). Understanding these elements is critical for developing new behaviors or modifying the frequency of existing ones. The behavioral process that describes relationships between events that have come before a behavior as well as the actual behavior during the acquisition of a new skill consists of the principles of shaping, discrimination, and generalization.

The shaping principle describes how one establishes respones that were previously not included in a student's behavioral repertoire. The discrimination principle describes how existing behaviors can come under control when new stimuli are added. The generalization principle describes how behavior in one environment under the presence of one stimulus can come under control of stimuli that are similar in a different environment.

For example, as one reviews shaping in terms of a vocational context, it is a reinforcement of vocational behaviors. Therefore, if an end goal is to clean one's work area, the person would necessarily need to know the steps for cleaning that area and concurrently be reinforced as he or she approached the completion of the desired work. Two extremely important strategies used in any shaping program that are often employed are task analysis and instructional programming.

Although task analysis was originally developed in the 1930s when industrial engineers were trying to improve the effectiveness and efficiency of work on extremely difficult tasks, the process has evolved into being an absolutely critical one in the vocational training of handicapped individuals. The process involves identification of all materials, movements, and responses of an existing task in a systematic way. One of the major applications of task analysis in vocational education was the development of an instructional sequence for training severely mentally retarded individuals to operate select tools (Crosson, 1969). This was soon followed by many applications such as those by Gold (1972) in which task analysis procedures were developed for the vocational training of mentally retarded persons to put together commercial types of materials.

The shaping principle is applied when one arranges and presents cues and consequences at the right time. These are often changed or modified so that the reinforcement of responses successfully approximate the type of end behavior one wishes (Rusch & Mithaug, 1980).

Instructional programming typically provides a set of procedures and materials that eventually lead to the development of new skills. Instructional procedures often include verbal instructions or cues, physical prompts, physical demonstrations, gestures, physical assistance, and guidance.

It is important when utilizing various cues to realize that there is a level of sophistication that is highly dependent upon the level of functioning of the trainee. For example, verbal cues, which are one of the highest levels of assistance, may be effective for mildly handicapped individuals, but may not be as effective for those in the severely and profoundly mentally retarded range. Verbal instruction also is not always effective with many adults who have been previously trained with gestural or physical prompts.

The generalization principle proposes that the more similar two or more events are, the more likely they will have similar effects on behavior. In training for generalization, it is important to pair the stimulus that controls the response with a second stimulus. Gradually, the first one is faded as the second one gains control over the behavior.

In summary, it is imperative that those working with handicapped individuals in the vocational programming area understand that training and management procedures rarely occur in isolation. It is also important to state that the interaction between the trainee's willingness to perform and a specified ability to perform is always a concern of the trainer. Often, a student may be willing but unable to perform a task because he or she does not know what is expected. In other cases, trainees may have the necessary skills but for some reason may be unwilling to perform the task. Obviously, what is needed is an analysis of each problem in terms of the essential components of an instructional process. Equally important is the assessment of the effects of different antecedent and consequent event arrangements as well as the ability of the student. Whatever approach is utilized, strategies must be selected that move the trainee toward vocational competence. When a student fails in an apparently obtainable skill, it may not only be his or her failure, but also the failure of the teacher or trainer to identify a correct strategy that will allow that individual to be successful.

EVALUATION

The initial stage of any training program is often referred to as an evaluation or assessment phase. It is directed at determining current client functioning as well as the potential for future vocational success. Vocational evaluation is a multifaceted process involving intake interviews, diagnostic testing, medical exams, and work assessments that utilize work samples and on-the-job training. Perhaps no one area is more critical in the vocational process, because vocational evaluation sets the scene or develops the foundation from where vocational programming begins.

For example, intake interviews not only provide social histories, but often provide significant information that may help to determine a specific component that should be added to the training program. Basic medical information as well as information concerning the cognitive domain is also critical at this stage especially as they relate to questions involving sensory problems or limitations, interests, and self-perceptions vis-à-vis vocational functioning. Work evaluation through on-the-job training can be utilized to assess student's work attitudes, behaviors, and skills related to the world of work.

The four-component evaluation process, which includes: (1) the intake interview; (2) a general medical exam; (3) an educational-psychological evaluation; and (4) a work evaluation, yields different types of information that may be used to develop a student's program. It is quickly apparent that the amount of relevant information gained will depend upon the type and severity of the disability and the skill level of the evaluator. For example, a nonverbal, severely/profoundly retarded individual may not provide much direct verbal information, but information can be obtained from observing the individual in a work or work sample situation.

Work Samples

Work samples allow a student to perform simulated or actual tasks that they may encounter in an actual work place. The students are evaluated on how well these tasks are performed. The work sample idea originated in the late 1930s with the development of the Tower System at the Institute for the Crippled and Disabled. In the 1950s federal legislation was passed that appropriated funds for the development of work sample evaluation techniques. Between the late 1960s and mid 1970s, several new systems were developed, including: the JEVS System devised by the Philadelphia Jewish Employment and Vocational Service, the VALPAR Component Work Samples Series, the Singer-Graflex Work Sample System, and the McCarron-Dial Work Evaluation System. Unfortunately, like most evaluation systems, it is often difficult to determine which system best fits a specific handicapped student's needs, and many systems or components remain inappropriate.

On-The-Job Evaluation

An on-the-job evaluation approach provides an assessment of an individual's abilities in an actual work situation. This focuses on how the client performs both attitudinally and in his or her ability to complete specific job tasks. In this situation, the student will receive supervision as if he or she were a regular employee of the company, although future employment is never assured.

Interpersonal Skill Training

It is not surprising that workshop surveys of employers continue to report that they require their clients to demonstrate appropriate social skills. In fact, the 10 most important skills identified by employers as being critical to "staying on the job" typically relate to acceptable interpersonal skill behaviors. The following list, developed by Rusch and Mithaug (1980), cites examples of critical behavior standards in vocational survival skills required by 90% or more of employers:

Employees should be able to:
1. Participate in work environments for 6-hour periods
2. Move safely about the shop by:

      a. Walking from place to place
      b. Identifying and avoiding dangerous areas
      c. Wearing safe work clothing
3. Work continuously at a job station for 1- to 2-hour periods
4. Learn new tasks when the supervisor explains by modeling
5. Come to work an average of five times per week
6. Correct work on a task after the second correction
7. Want to work for money/sense of accomplishment
8. Understand work routine by not displaying disruptive behavior during routine program changes
9. Continue to work without disruption when:
      a. Supervisor is observing
      b. Fellow worker is observing
      c. Stranger is observing
10. Adapt to new work environment with normal levels of productivity in 1 to 5 days and with normal levels of contact with supervisor in 30 to 60 minutes.

Note: From *Vocational Training for Mentally Retarded Adults* (p. 115) by F. R. Rusch and D. E. Mithaug, 1980, Champaign, IL: Research Press. Copyright 1980 by Research Press. Reprinted by permission.

In addition, Valletutti and Bender (1982) have developed a system of behavioral objectives that address the teaching of work-related interpersonal skills, including:

    A.   ***Looking and Applying for Work***
    B.   ***Getting Ready for Work***
    C.   ***Going to Work***
    D.   ***Work Rules and Policies***
    E.   ***Work Breaks***
    F.   ***On-the-job Skills***
    G.   ***Compensation for Work***

The following are examples of each area:

A. *Looking and Applying For Work*

The individual:

1. contacts job placement bureaus (public and private) for information.
2. calls friends or acquaintances who may know about job opportunities.

3. reviews newspapers containing help wanted sections for prospective jobs.
4. applies for job(s) specific to skills, training, qualifications, and interests.
5. provides necessary and pertinent job and personal information to prospective employer.
6. arranges for a job interview.
7. prepares for a job interview.
8. attends job interviews.
9. interviews for job(s) specific to skills, training, qualifications, and interests.
10. discusses training, work experiences, interests, and other pertinent information with prospective employers.
11. follows up job interview with a phone call or letter if the result of interview within the time frame specified by prospective employer is not known.
12. resumes job search when previous attempts at seeking employment have not met with success.
13. signs necessary forms and documents when successful in obtaining employment, and purchases required equipment, materials, and clothing.
14. supplies needed verification documents including birth certificate, citizenship papers, and work permits.
15. obtains a physical examination when required and arranges for results to be reported to the employer.

B. Getting Ready for Work

The individual:

1. makes arrangements to arise on time for work (i.e., setting alarm clock or clock radio and arranging for wake-up calls).
2. uses bathroom facilities, at predetermined times, whenever possible.
3. grooms himself or herself appropriately while getting ready for work.
4. maintains own privacy and respects privacy of others while dressing for work.
5. dresses appropriately and neatly for specific job and weather conditions.
6. participates in morning conversations with peers, family members, or acquaintances when appropriate and when there is sufficient time.

7. prepares and eats a meal and cleans up before going to work.
8. prepares and packs meals or snacks for on-the-job breaks and scheduled mealtimes.
9. checks to make sure that the materials, money, and/or food needed for work are ready.
10. checks to make sure that the correct change, tokens, tickets, or passes for transportation to work are available.

C. *Going to Work*

The individual:

1. leaves residence in time to arrive at work at scheduled starting time or earlier.
2. meets buses, car pools, and/or shuttle services on schedule.
3. greets bus drivers and car pool members as appropriate.
4. tells taxi driver exact location of work and pays correct fare plus an appropriate tip.
5. makes alternate arrangements for transportation to work when bus, shuttle services, or routine rides are missed.
6. makes alternate arrangements for transportation when routine transportation systems are not operating.
7. interacts in car pool discussions when appropriate.
8. pays share of transportation cost when participating as a passenger in car pools.
9. provides assistance to driver as needed (e.g., following detour signs, reading maps, and getting tolls ready).
10. greets doorman, security guards, elevator operators, etc. upon arriving at work.

D. *Work Rules and Policies*

The individual:

1. calls employer when he or she cannot report to work or is going to be late.
2. requests clarification of work rules from employer if uncertain about specific rules or if there has been a change in rules or policies.
3. obeys health rules pertinent to his or her job.
4. obeys safety rules relative to safe job behaviors (e.g., "Wear Protective Clothing" and "Wear Protective Glasses").
5. obeys safety signs of prohibition, such as "No Smoking" and "No Food."

6. follows verbal cautions and suggestions made by fellow employees whenever appropriate.
7. obeys fire drill rules and procedures during fires, drills, and other times of building evacuation.
8. discusses work problems with immediate supervisor.
9. discusses emergency health problems with company nurse, medical personnel, or other appropriate designee.
10. respects and does not interfere with other workers' property.
11. respects other workers' privacy.
12. maintains work areas in a neat and acceptable manner.
13. reports equipment in need of repair, parts that need replacing, and tools not operating properly, to appropriate supervisor.
14. cleans and arranges work area for the next day's work.

E. On-the-Job Skills

The individual:

1. performs those motor skills necessary for carrying out special assignments.
2. shares key information found in memos and directions with fellow workers (when appropriate).
3. uses tools, equipment, and materials properly.
4. conserves materials by using them efficiently.
5. follows the posted rules and/or procedures for returning tools and unused materials to tool rooms and sheds.
6. works cooperatively with co-workers in carrying out job tasks.

Work Breaks

The individual:

1. participates in taking a break during break time.
2. asks co-workers for directions to restrooms, telephones, exits, entrances, snack bars, and cafeterias.
3. discusses information found on bulletin boards with co-workers during leisure breaks.
4. participates, on a voluntary basis, in work or sports pools.
5. asks fellow workers for change to use in vending machines when exact change is not available.
6. participates, on a voluntary basis, in treating co-workers to beverages and/or snacks during break or other appropriate times.
7. does not spread rumors heard from co-workers.

8. obeys time limits or breaks and reports back to work immediately after the break is over.
9. engages in conversation with fellow workers when appropriate.
10. participates in planning for company leisure activities such as picnics, bowling leagues, and baseball outings.
11. plans recreational activities with co-workers.

G. *Compensation for Work*

The individual:

1. discusses any problem with paycheck with appropriate supervisor.
2. cashes paycheck at a bank, supermarket, or store frequented.
3. opens a savings account in a credit union or bank.
4. opens up a checking account and uses it for depositing a portion of his or her salary for payment of bills.
5. decides whether or not a portion of pay should be deducted for any charities (i.e., United Fund).
6. designates specific amount of pay for union dues, medical coverage, life insurance, etc.

It is clear that vocational training should not just focus upon special tasks being taught, but also upon interpersonal skill development. Both are necessary for successful career development and integration of the handicapped into the community. Obviously, this emphasis means a reanalysis of some commonly held beliefs: that task training is paramount and that interpersonal skills can be learned on the job.

JOB AND ENVIRONMENTAL MODIFICATION

The modification of a job is a process through which one adapts, redistributes, or eliminates tasks from a job. A key point in this process is that no matter how a job is changed or modified, it must be performed effectively.

For years we have heard of the potential disadvantages of some environmental modifications. Perhaps most notable are the increased costs to business as well as the possibility that some types of jobs can be so oversimplified that they become monotonous and routine to the handicapped worker. As a result, laws that support the modification of environmental conditions for the handicapped constantly have been reviewed and assessed from a cost/benefit basis.

Today, however, job modifications are increasing and vocational training efforts have greatly benefited from the technology that has been made available through engineering and science. This is especially true for those handicapped individuals with severe to profound limitations where job restructuring and environmental modifications are a necessity. Unfortunately, not everyone involved in the vocational training process has access to personnel with expertise in job modification. However, those who do have this resource appear to develop programs that are relevant and functional for the handicapped population they are training.

It is important to note that environmental modification is not only a process that aids handicapped individuals by altering their physical surroundings (i.e., ramps or curbs that have been lowered), but also includes modifications that involve the attitudinal domain, which seems to be much more difficult to alter.

It is now clear that one of the best and most effective ways of improving or changing attitudes in the vocational area is to insist that the handicapped individual perform his or her job in an exemplary and expeditious manner.

CONCLUSION

For those who have worked at length in vocational rehabilitation or habilitation of the handicapped it is accurate to say that their goal is the successful placement and employment of their clients. It is also now apparent that instructors must not only assess the client but also assess and understand other environmental influences, such as: (1) possible job sites; (2) availability of technology; (3) career potential; (4) changing job markets; and (5) the possibility that many existing jobs might require modification or restructuring to allow for the inclusion of handicapped workers.

Whether one takes the approach that trains handicapped students *before* they are placed in prospective jobs or the approach that trains students "on-the-job" is not as important as addressing the overriding issue that handicapped individuals are indeed entitled to job training. Placements for severely handicapped workers also must include a continuum that goes from preworkshop placement to some form of gainful employment.

Even though the sheltered workshop has had a changing role within the last two decades, it has not changed enough. The majority of these institutions provide very little in the way of integrating handicapped workers into the community (Pomerantz & Marholian, 1977) and offer little in the way of career incentives. (Unfortunately, most also generally fail to take advantage of assistance from service groups outside their program administration and often fail to see the relevance of resources within a community.) For too long, we have allowed severely handicapped individuals to be placed in unidimensional programs such as sheltered workshops. This observation does not mean that we do not need sheltered workshops, but rather that these types of programs are often too limiting and provide little in the way of a variety of vocational and career options.

Any type of training for the handicapped must be expeditiously accomplished and carefully selected to include screening and interviewing, vocational evaluation, job exploration, and interpersonal skill and on-the-job training. Much of this will eventually be done through computer technology. We must also realize that traditional diagnostic testing does not effectively or completely evaluate work potential; handicapped individuals have taught us that they can achieve, given equal opportunity for appropriate training.

The presence and availability of personal computers opens new doors for the handicapped. Vocational training programs have now begun to include computer technology as part of their teaching methodology, which ultimately may help the handicapped to explore careers, find jobs, and learn work skills not before thought possible.

The chapters that follow present information and new hope for this often ignored population of individuals.

REFERENCES

Bender, M. (1978). Teaching through imitation: Industrial education for the moderately and severely retarded. *Journal of Education and Training of the Mentally Retarded*, 13(1), 16–21.

Bender, M., & Valletutti, P. (1976–1977). *Teaching the moderately and severely handicapped* (3 vols.). Austin: PRO-ED.

Bender, M., & Valletutti, P. (1982). *Teaching functional academics: A curriculum guide for adolescents and adults with learning problems.* Austin: PRO-ED.

Crosson, J. (1969). A technique for programming sheltered workshop environments for training severely retarded workers. *American Journal of Mental Deficiency, 73*, 814–818.

Gold, M. (1972). Stimulus factors in skill training of retarded adolescents on a complex assembly task: Acquisition, transfer, and retention. *American Journal of Mental Deficiency, 76*, 517–526.

Hansen, C., & Haring, N. (1980). *Expanding opportunities: Vocational education for the handicapped.* Seattle: University of Washington.

Lynch, K. P. (1979). Toward a skill-oriented prevocational program for trainable and severely mentally impaired students. In G. T. Bellamy, G. O'Connor, & O. C. Karan (Eds.), *Vocational rehabilitation of severely handicapped persons: Contemporary service strategies.* Austin: PRO-ED.

Pomerantz, D., & Marholin, D. (1977). Vocational habilitation: A time for change in existing service delivery systems. In E. Sontag, N. Certo, & J. Smith

3

The Application of Career Development Theory to the Handicapped

Donald E. Super

The origins of career development theory lie in the study of typical samples of the general population. It has long been known that development is the result of interaction between an organism and its environment. Both the individual and the environment bring essential components to this process.

Organisms have potentials that are realized only if the environment permits, and only to the degree that organism and environment permit it. Thus, in considering the career development of the handicapped, our focus must be on the development of their potential. It is important to recognize when focusing on learning, physical, and mental handicaps that they are not all in one category. Handicapping conditions may be developmental or accidental or some combination of the two. For example, learning disabilities and physical handicaps are sometimes developmental and sometimes accidental, whereas mental retardation is usually congenital, or at least develops at an early age. Accidents such as brain damage and spinal injuries can cause disabilities at any age, disabilities that did not exist prior to the accident, illness, or trauma.

Developmental handicaps, whether physical or mental, involve less trauma psychologically and thus, in some ways, cause less damage to the career development of an individual than do accidental handicaps. Once the nature of the handicap is understood, provisions can be taken to minimize, as much as possible, the impact of the handicap on the individual.

Exposure to the real world emerges as a crucial factor in the career development of the developmentally handicapped. Growing up without normal ability to see, hear, read, speak, walk, or do what their advantaged peers can do, the disabled miss many opportunities for both incidental and planned learning. For example, Lerman (1966) found that deaf students achieved lower scores on measures of planning ability, exploration, and knowledge of career development and occupational opportunities than did normal hearing pupils of the same age. Isolated from the "real world," they saw, read, and even heard less about it, and had less experience in coping with it during vacation or part-time jobs. They also had less opportunity for learning vicariously through the dinner table conversation with parents or older siblings in the general labor force. The same lack of exposure to the real world has been observed, although not so well assessed, in the visually, motorically, and verbally handicapped. What Lerman found is worth repeating: Developmental handicaps mean limited opportunities to explore the world of work, limited stimulus to anticipate career development tasks and to plan ahead, limited accumulation of knowledge of what may lie ahead in the way of career decisions and actions, and limited awareness of the occupational opportunities that may await. Special schools studied by Kent (1982) did what they could to make up for the handicaps of the mentally retarded and helped them encounter the real world in a guided or even sheltered way; whereas in mainstream schools, the mentally retarded did not receive the special help needed to minimize their handicap.

What has been said about mental retardation could also be said about physical disabilities that exist at or soon after birth, for here, too, opportunity to interact with the real world is often limited. Cerebral palsied children may be unable to circulate as their peers do and may even have the handicap exaggerated by teachers and fellow students and thus be shut out of some experiences that would be beneficial. The cardiac child, although perhaps not viewed as handicapped by teachers and peers, may have fears and attitudes that are just as limiting as those that might result from a visible handicap.

The learning disabilities cannot be so easily categorized, because some are probably due to special factors such as brain injury or to limited or misdirected educational experiences. However, whether congenital or experiential, of early or of late onset, disabilities have the effect of limiting interaction with the real world as experienced through books, motion pictures, television, conversation, and actual work. As in the case of the deaf, the disability often results in less exploratory behavior, less planning, and less information about careers and about occupations.

Accidental handicaps may also be of early or of late onset, like learning disabilities and physical handicaps. But *un*like mental retardation, and *like* most learning disabilities and many physical handicaps, accidental handicaps most often result from an illness or an injury, such as a bad fall or a collision, after normal development has progressed to a certain point. Deafness and blindness, as in the often-reported case of Helen Keller, are handicaps in which potential can be discovered and a deficit of experience can be overcome in a way that, if properly handled, can be as inspirational as it is frustrating. However, becoming deaf and/or blind at age 10, 30, or 50 has a completely different impact on the individual. The loss of contact is traumatic, and the period of mourning the loss may be long and difficult, but skills already learned visually and auditorally provide a basis for relearning that greatly facilitates the retraining process, especially when aids such as programmed microcomputers are available. Once the willingness to use newly acquired aids such as books or keys in braille, hand pressure, and guide dogs has been developed, the knowledge of the real world gained while able to see and hear can be drawn on to develop substitute skills and additional knowledge and understanding. The adolescent or adult who has been accidentally handicapped also has a prior fund of knowledge of the real world that can be enriched by the use of the substitute skills, whereas the person with a childhood handicap has no such frame of reference, no such "apperceptive mass," in which to fit newly acquired knowledge. Unless helped by a tutor or computer, the handicapped individual may not even know what questions to ask, much less how to organize the information acquired.

Continuity and discontinuity of development are thus different in different types of physically and mentally handicapped people. Career development theory has tended to stress continuity in development, and middle-class bias has made it easy for many theorists, teachers, and counselors to assume that most careers are continuous (i.e., conventional or stable). A conventional career, in the languages of occupational sociology and vocational psychology, is a career in which, after a limited amount of trial in entry- and low-level jobs, individuals move up to and settle down in for most of their adult working lives. A stable career is one in which people obtain their related training, enter an occupation for which that training has prepared them, move ahead in it, settle into a permanent job, and, in due course, retire from it. Vocational guidance, having been conceived and developed by educators and people who value education, has tended to advocate this middle-class view of careers. They tend to think of the desirable career as one in which, with a minimum of change of direction, the individual moves toward a goal, attains that goal, and, on finding it satisfactory, enjoys the continuing pursuit of this activity.

As has been historically pointed out (Hollingshead, 1949; LoCascio, 1964; Miller & Form, 1951; Super, 1957), however, large numbers of men and women do not pursue continuous careers. Instead, they pursue discontinuous careers in which the occupation pursued at one period in their lives has no relationship to one pursued at some other period. Discontinuous careers have been broken down into multiple-trial careers in which a number of differing occupations are pursued in seemingly random succession and unstable careers in which a period of stabilization in one occupation or industry is followed by a period in another unrelated field of work, which in turn may be followed by employment in another unrelated occupation.

Data on the relative frequency of these career patterns with the handicapped is lacking, but it seems likely that accidentally handicapped adults have unstable careers with significantly greater frequency than other adults because, although once established in one job or occupation, their postaccident job often must be different and is attainable only after retraining.

One major change of jobs may be the only change in such cases, for it may be that, once retrained and reemployed, the victim of the accident may hold onto his or her job and perform more diligently than an advantaged person. This is often true of persons with long-term, congenital, or early childhood handicaps. Indeed, one would expect these individuals to resemble other types of handicapped persons, for at this life stage, each group has had time to adjust to and to some degree overcome the handicap.

Career development theory has made much use of life stage theory (e.g., Buehler, 1933; Super, 1957), enriched by developmental task theory (Havighurst, 1953). As used by some writers (e.g., Levinson, 1978) with a Piagetian, biological orientation, life stage theory implies or even specifies a preordained, genetically programmed sequence of stages. Each stage with roughly predetermined ages of entry and of exit, must be gone through before the next can be entered. However, in his formulation of developmental task theory Havighurst writes of the *importance*, not the *inevitability*, of progressing through each stage and accomplishing its developmental tasks in order that the next set of tasks can be well handled. Thus, the childhood task of developing a self-concept helps, if handled well, in the making of curricular and preoccupational choices in adolescence,. and helps also with the continuing development of a self-concept modified appropriately for coping with the needs and demands of adolescence and emerging adulthood. If the self-concept of a given life stage is unrealistic, insufficiently refined, or unclear, the other tasks of that life stage and of later stages are likely to be mishandled.

Developmental task theory has important implications for the career development of the handicapped. A first implication is obvious: A handicap makes it more difficult for the individual to cope with the environmentally imposed task, for he or she has less opportunity than advantaged people to understand social expectations, to internalize the attitudes of others without damage to self-concepts, and to acquire information essential to good decision making.

A second implication is, as Kent (1982) showed, that special provisions need to be made to provide encounters with the environment, encounters that contribute to understanding the self and the environment. These provisions need to go beyond providing the encounters. They need also to help in the handling and evaluation of the importance of the experiences provided. This calls for instruction before and after the encounter and help in handling its emotional impact.

Developmental theory deals not just with developmental tasks, but with the transitions for which they prepare the individual. There is the transition from child at home to pupil in school, with greater independence typical of the latter. There is the transition from pupil to student as the high school youth learns to do homework without supervision, and from child to youth with pubescence and dating. There is the transition from dependent youth to independent adult, itself followed by the transition to interdependent adult with the establishment of a new family in a new home, and the transition from person with limited responsibility and that only for him or herself, to a person fully responsible for his or her own actions and, at times, for the safety, behavior, or development of others. Microcomputers with interactive programs can make it possible for the handicapped to role play these transitions.

Handicapped people are, by definition, people not as well equipped as most to cope with the tasks of transition. The ability to anticipate future events and conditions, understand how to deal with them, and act accordingly is affected by the handicap.

Having a physical or mental handicap deprives one of access to certain kinds of information about the world and about one's own functioning in it. Comments about one's actions cannot be heard by the deaf, facial reactions of others cannot be seen by the blind, and, more fundamental, situations and people often cannot be encountered by the severely orthopedically impaired. Observations of the world of work, whether achieved vicariously as in motion pictures and books or in person as in plant visits and cooperative employment, are limited if one's communication and transportation skills are limited. In this sense, the handicapped are deprived of experiences and insights that are available to others. They are therefore disadvantaged.

IMPLICATIONS FOR PRACTICE

Because the core of the career development problems of the handicapped is their limited communication capacity, whether the limitations are visual, auditory, spoken, or motoric, the implications for helping them with these problems are implications for finding better ways of communication with and for them. These must include exposing handicapped individuals to opportunities for learning about the world of work and to ways in which they might fit into it for the maximum realization of their potential.

For the handicapped, then, as for the advantaged, basic skills are important. Mastery of these may be different from that of sighted, hearing, speaking, and ambulatory persons but some sort of mastery training is needed. So, given a sound approach to basic skills, what next?

Both shelter and exposure are needed. Special provisions for exposure to the real world need to be made, while sheltering the handicapped from demands that exceed their current capacity to respond effectively. The original concept of the sheltered workshop is a familiar one, and while it is *not* what is proposed here for all handicapped persons, some of the original workshop concepts (i.e., graduated experiences tailored to the readiness of the individual for the experience, whether in simulation or in real life) are worth considering. As with independence training for children and adolescents, too little too late is bad, and too much too soon is bad: The readiness of the individual must be taken into account, and the experience planned accordingly. There must be normal opportunity to fail, but with it, reasonable chances of succeeding.

Given the basic skills of communication, opportunities to use them can be provided in the familiar ways of career education and adapted to the capacities of the individual. In particular, role models—people who can help bridge the reality gap between books, cassettes, filmstrips, talks, video games, and computers, on the one hand, and the three-dimensional world on the other—are important. Role models are most effective when: 1) there is direct personal contact between modeler and model; and 2) when the student shadows an adult performing a pertinent type of work, with opportunity for occasional questions, explanations, and discussion (as in organized work experience in which the counselee is given the opportunity to perform a certain kind of work in a situation in which he or she can interact with experienced workers doing and supervising that kind of work in their daily routines). Of course, before such experience can be provided without too much trial and error, the classroom, laboratory, lecture hall and computerized methods need to be tailored to the handicaps of the person or persons experiencing the orientation process.

Counseling does not occur in a vacuum, self-understanding does not happen without feedback from reality, and choices cannot be made without knowledge of real options. The career development of the handicapped requires orientation by means of information conveyed in effective ways through a variety of human and technological media that are still being developed.

REFERENCES

Buehler, C. *Der menchliche lebensdorf als psychologisches Problem.* Leipsig: Hirzel, 1933.

Havighurst, R. J. (1953). *Human development and education.* New York: Longman's Green.

Hollingshead, A. B. (1949). *Elmtown's youth.* New York: Wiley.

Kent, A. J. (1982). Occupational choice in slow-learning school leavers. Unpublished master's dissertation, The Hatfield Polytechnic, Hertford (England).

Lerman, A. (1966). A study of contributors to vocational choice in deaf adolescents. Unpublished doctoral dissertation, New York University, New York.

Levinson, D. J. *The Seasons of a Man's Life.* New York: Ballentine, 1978.

LoCascio, R. (1964). The vocational maturity of diverse groups. In D. E. Super (Ed.), *Measuring vocational maturity for counseling and evaluation.* Washington, DC: National Vocational Guidance Association.

Miller, D. C., & Form, W. H. (1951). *Industrial sociology.* New York: Harper.

Super, D. E. (1957). The psychology of careers. New York: Harper.

4

Career Education for the Handicapped

Marion V. Panyan and Gail McGregor

The scope and purpose of career education for handicapped persons has broadened significantly in recent years. Contemporary career education efforts reflect both an ecological and a longitudinal process that emphasizes the various settings significant in an individual's daily life (Brolin, 1977; U.S. Department of Health, Education, and Welfare, 1975). Thus, the coordination of home, school, and community components is viewed as critical in terms of coordinating the environments in which an individual currently and subsequently functions. From a career education perspective, course offerings and work experiences must be evaluated on the basis of their contribution in enabling students to: (1) develop the ability to choose alternative careers; (2) acquire marketable job skills; and (3) function adequately in the world of work. Although the concept of career education is comprehensive in scope, it focuses on the integration of educational experiences aimed at preparing the student for adult life. Not only are vocational skills stressed under the rubric of career education, adequate preparation for careers in the home and community is emphasized as well.

There is a current push in educational programs for the handicapped to increase each person's independence in community, home, school, recreational, and vocational settings. All instructional objectives, materials, skills, and tasks are evaluated in terms of their *functional* importance (Reichle, Williams, Volgelsberg, & Williams, 1980). Academic subject matter that does not further daily living and work skills is deleted and replaced by chronologically age-appropriate training skills that will enable the handicapped to contribute to whatever extent possible

(Brown, Falvey, Vincent, Kaye, Johnson, Ferrara-Parish, & Gruenewald, 1980). Thus, career education is best viewed as a common, unifying foundation for traditional academic subjects, vocational education, and independent living skill training (D'Alonzo, 1977).

COMPONENTS OF CAREER EDUCATION PROGRAMS

The identification of key competencies and outcomes is the first step in designing effective career education programs for the handicapped. Fortunately, comprehensive lists of career development competencies that are critical for community functioning are available (Brolin, 1978; Sprafkin, Gershaw, & Goldstein, 1978; Walls, Zane & Werner, 1979). Brolin's list included 22 skills, along with personal-social skills and occupational guidance and preparation. The objectives of Walls et al. (1979), on the other hand, specify clear standards for determining vocational competence in the different areas of prevocational skills, job-seeking skills, interview skills, job-related skills, work performance skills, on-the-job social skills, and union, financial, and security skills. Although these competencies may be appropriate for 1984, additions and/or revisions will most likely be required in the future or when skills are referenced to a specific local community (Wilcox & Bellamy, 1982). An inventory of present and projected needs in terms of one's home community will take into account societal and economic factors as well as the local job market, helping to identify those skills and attitudes critical to success in a targeted community.

Once competencies have been identified, a plan or program enabling students to achieve the stated objectives needs to be designed and implemented. At the individual level, the nucleus of this program is the student's individualized education program (IEP), individualized program plan (IPP), or individualized written rehabilitation program (IWRP). Quality services, however, are not ensured by merely preparing these documents adequately. Many current service delivery systems exhibit shortcomings that significantly compromise the effectiveness of training for the handicapped population in general. These limitations include the type of student served, the length of time a student is served, and the setting in which a student is served.

LIMITATIONS OF CONTEMPORARY VOCATIONAL EDUCATION PROGRAMS

Traditionally, vocational education programs for the handicapped have focused on individuals with mild or moderate retardation (Becker,

Widener, & Soforenko, 1979). The inclusion of only higher functioning individuals in these training programs was based on two erroneous assumptions. One assumption was that the prospect of gainful employment must be apparent to the trainer at the outset of instruction. The second error was the assumption that competitive employment is the only goal of training, thereby precluding efforts with those individuals who may not achieve this goal. If one considers the implication of this vocational education philosophy, it is clear that services and instruction were and are denied to the very individuals who need them most. Recent programs involving moderately and severely handicapped individuals (Bellamy, Sheehan, Horner, & Boles, 1980; Brickey & Campbell, 1981; Sowers, Thompson, & Connis, 1979; Wehman, Hill, & Koehler, 1979) illustrate the employment potential of this population when provided with adequate, longitudinal training. It is hoped that they will serve to weaken these long-held views.

A second limitation of many current vocational education programs is that they are first instituted at the secondary level (D'Alonzo, 1977). A more recent trend espoused by career education is exposing a student to a variety of career options as early as possible. Kokaska's (1978) model of progressing from career awareness (K–6), to career exploration (7–8), orientation (9–10), and finally preparation (11–12) is somewhat applicable here. However, certain characteristics of mentally retarded individuals, particularly delays in cognitive and social-emotional development, are not compatible with this timetable. Elements from all phases of career education should be presented earlier and longer than at the grades delineated by Kokaska. For example, an excellent guide and set of programming strategies for career education for elementary age students is provided by Clark (1979).

A third weakness of current vocational education programs for the handicapped is the lack of integration or "mainstreaming" with regular vocational students (Budke, Bettis, & Beasley, 1972). In some instances, minor modifications in the work environment or the task itself can ensure a handicapped individual easy access to the same opportunities and challenges afforded to regular students. Nevertheless, Halloran (1978) reported that only 1.7% of the students enrolled in vocational education programs in fiscal year 1975 were identified as handicapped. These figures, coupled with inadequate postschool services, show that the handicapped fail not because of innate deficiencies but because of inadequate service systems.

In view of the limitations just enumerated, it is not surprising that many students are unprepared to enter and succeed in selected careers. Some 2.5 million nonhandicapped students leave the formal education system yearly without adequate preparation for a career (Mori, 1979). A depressed economy and a high national unemployment rate only further exacerbate the problem. The situation is even more bleak for handicapped students: 80% of the handicapped population leaving school in any one year are unemployed (Bureau of Education for the Handicapped, 1975). Community attitudes also constitute a major roadblock for handicapped students on the way to employment and community integration. Although the research literature is replete with evidence that the handicapped can learn job skills (Brickey & Campbell, 1981; Clark, 1979; Wehman, Hill, Goodall, Cleveland, Brooke, & Pentecost, 1982), societal acceptance and accommodation of them in the labor force show that it is not always just the handicapped who need to adapt or change.

A survey (U.S. Department of Labor Employment Standards Administration, 1982) of private sector employees contracting with the federal government gathered information regarding the accommodation practices for handicapped employees demonstrated by these companies. It was found that approximately 50% of the respondents reported either no handicapped workers or no efforts to accommodate handicapped workers. In those firms that had hired handicapped employees, the cost of accommodations was relatively small. Fifty-one percent of these companies reported necessary accommodations were made at no cost and 30% reported costs less than $500, whereas only 8% reported costs exceeding $2,000. The most frequently cited impediments to hiring the handicapped included the lack of skills of many handicapped applicants, making accommodation an "uncertain investment," and the perception that some work sites were inherently too unsafe for accommodation to be feasible.

EXEMPLARY PROGRAMS AND STRATEGIES

Given such conditions and attitudes, one might question the very existence of career education programs for the handicapped. Despite the generally negative climate and shortage of funds for such programs, we propose that the basic intent and concepts of career education programs must pervade all educational programs. Efforts to implement such programs should be increased and upgraded rather than diminished. More intensive training should prepare the students to contribute to their home and community to the fullest extent possible. In short, career education programs should train their graduates to live productively as well as to make a productive living.

There are positive signs in society at large, and in our educational system and community services in particular, which might provide the impetus to reverse the present situation. Legislation mandating appropriate vocational experiences, such as the 1976 Amendments to the Vocational Educational Act (P.L. 94-482, *U.S. Federal Register,* October 3, 1977), the Vocational Rehabilitation Act of 1973 (P.L. 93-112, *U.S. Federal Register,* May 4, 1977), and the Education for All Handicapped Children Act of 1975 (P.L. 94-142, *U.S. Federal Register,* August 23, 1977), has prompted new and better services for handicapped students.

A search through Resources in Vocational Education (RIVE) yielded 19 citations of innovative comprehensive career education projects for the mentally retarded. A major lifelong career development project is underway in Columbia, Missouri, to develop a prototypic model and inservice training package using the community college as the central coordinating agency (Flanagan & Schoepke, 1978). Juhrs (1982) reported the successful placement of previously institutionalized autistic adults in competitive employment situations. These programs and others like them conduct training in the least restrictive environment and generally respond to the intent of recent legislation.

The application of behavioral principles to the training of the handicapped (Bijou, 1970) provides educators with an instructional technology that has an impressive track record, particularly with difficult-to-manage students. Systematic use of behavioral principles could substantially further the attainment of career education objectives. Finally, the technological revolution that has encompassed society as a whole is having a rapid impact on our schools (Tawney & Cartwright, 1981). Microcomputers and other associated hardware and peripheral devices seem to hold great potential in their applications in special education (Eisele, 1980; Taber, 1983). Thus, the remaining discussion focuses on both the instructional and electronic technology available to special educators involved in career education with handicapped students. It is our contention that, collectively, these two technologies have the potential to improve career education efforts with handicapped individuals.

Behavioral Technology

The applied behavior analysis approach has been singularly successful in teaching handicapped persons to become more independent and self-sufficient. It is beyond the scope of this chapter to provide a comprehensive treatment of either the strategies involved in the behavioral approach or the outcomes it has produced. Behavioral strategies have been successfully described by Kazdin (1980) and extended to vocational programming by Rusch and Mithaug (1980). Based on the work of Snell

(1978) and Tawney, Knapp, O'Reilly, and Pratt (1979), Tawney and Cartwright (1981) operationalized the behavioral principles in a set of "best practices" of contemporary instructional technology. These strategies include:

1. Defining what is taught.
   a. Stating the conditions of instruction.
   b. Response specification.
   c. Stating criterion performance.
2. Careful analysis of prerequisite skills.
3. Precise behavioral assessment.
4. Precise skill or content analysis.
5. Fine-grain instructional sequencing—or programming for errorless learning.
   a. Specification of teacher statements, cues, and prompts.
   b. Specification of correction procedures.
   c. Use of reinforcer systems.
6. Data-based instruction—immediate decision-making based on student's correct and error responses.
7. Empirical verification of the effects of an educational intervention.
8. Direct and daily measurement of student responses.
9. Defined decision rules for program branching or program modification.
10. Systematic programming through all phases of learning; acquisition, proficiency, maintenance, and generalization. (Tawney & Cartwright, 1981, p. 6)

When instruction is provided in this manner, each student's learning potential and accomplishments are maximized. However, the behavioral approach is not without practical obstacles, as when a classroom teacher is faced with six or more students, each of whom requires a number of such structured programs requiring constant monitoring and adjustment. Microcomputers potentially represent a method for providing all students with individualized self-paced programs.

MICROCOMPUTER TECHNOLOGY

Microcomputers can assist teachers in providing quality educational programs, given an instructional setting where sound curriculum and teaching practices are evidenced. It is important to stress at the outset, however, that a computer is only a machine through which programs are run. Without adequate software, the computer may only interfere with the instructional process. To be an effective educational tool, programs must adhere to instructional design principles (Gagne & Briggs, 1979) and teaching procedures enumerated earlier by Tawney et al. (1981).

Microcomputer-based instruction has the potential to create individualized learning opportunities by teaching different content in different ways to different students. Via the computer, students are able to receive information at their own rate of speed, presented in a way that matches their "cognitive style" (Cosky, 1980). The machine's capabilities of combining sound, color, and graphics enable stimuli to be both captivating, and individually tailored in regard to the salience of a particular input modality. Furthermore, a programming feature called "branching" allows the sequence of instructional material presented to the student to be individually geared to his or her performance each day. Thus, if a designated number of errors are made in a row, a program can "branch" to a section providing more assistance in the content area causing difficulty for the student.

A more recent technological enhancement is the combination of microcomputers with videodiscs (Allard & Thorkildsen, 1981). The videodisc has a capacity of 54,000 individual frames of color photographic display and is capable of being controlled by microcomputers in presenting and overlaying simultaneous instructional material on the screen (Eisele, 1981). The possibilities in applications with nonreading handicapped individuals are multiple because instruction can also be provided through the audio track of the videodisc. The Intelligent Videodisc for Special Education Technology project currently underway at Utah State University (Allard & Thorkildsen, 1981) is a preliminary investigation of the application of this technology with moderately to severely retarded individuals. Project staff have developed instructional packages for training content such as Time Telling, Coin Recognition, Functional Word Recognition, and Matching, all of which may be a necessary part of an individual's total career education program.

Another capability of microcomputers that reflects a concern for an individual's unique needs is providing alternative response modes. The addition of any number of peripheral devices (e.g., single-switch inputs, touch panels, voice-activated inputs, and touch-sensitive screens) would seem to preclude any individual being excluded from using this technology because of the lack of an appropriate interface mechanism. For those individuals unable to use a traditional keyboard, single-switch inputs can easily be added to microcomputers. However, there are only a handful of available programs that are written to accept single-switch inputs. One recent development that may help to remedy this situation is the commercial marketing of an adaptive firmware card (Schwejda & Vanderheiden, 1983). The addition of this firmware card to a regular Apple II or Apple IIe provides the user with a variety of input routines, including scanning, Morse code, and direct selection, that can be used in conjunction with commercial software not originally written to accept switch input. A second alternative for those capable of speech is a Voice Input Module (MCE, 1983). This peripheral allows the user to speak isolated words or phrases in order to provide the computer with commands.

A results-oriented program focuses on outcomes (i.e., whether the student masters the task or whether the student answers questions appropriately). The computer is an impartial judge of student responses. Immediate feedback can advise the student of the adequacy of the response. Planned instructional contingencies displayed by the computer consist of three options: (1) sequential progress to advanced materials or stimuli when the response is adequate; (2) repetition of the materials or stimuli when the response is inappropriate; or (3) branching to new materials for enrichment or remediation (Eisele, 1980). Branching is the only option that readily ensures individualization; it is a desirable feature in software programs. Finally, the computer has the capability of introducing new means of achieving the targeted objectives when previous methods have been unsuccessful.

The emphasis on continuous measurement is the defining characteristic of behavior analysis, and is directly related to the focus on results. Likewise, the computer has the capability of keeping ongoing records of student performance. The scoring/recording of student performance is just one of the information management functions that is the responsibility of teachers. The computer is also capable of assisting in the development and monitoring of student IEPs as well as in the preparation of written reports. All three activities are critical yet time-consuming functions that can be greatly simplified with computer technology.

FUTURE PERSPECTIVES

In order for microcomputers to complement the teacher in the task of providing quality education, two conditions must be met. The first condition is the availability and selection of appropriate software. The second condition is an informed and receptive staff. It is clear that hardware development has far surpassed the development of quality software for educational purposes, particularly regarding applications with handicapped learners. It is also apparent that computers have inundated schools at a rate that has led some to exhibit a reaction coined "computerphobia" (Jay, 1981). The following examination of current and future practices involving microcomputer-based instruction focuses on these two important issues: software and staff attitudes and training.

Software

If the number of publishing companies adding computer software to their product line is a valid indicator, the available market in computer software is growing geometrically. Organizations concerned with education on the local and national levels are quickly responding to a common concern that much of the available software is not educationally sound. As a result, software review committees are being established that use stringent evaluation criteria to assess new products. A number of suggested evaluation criteria are also readily available to computer users to assist them in their personal selections (Hannaford & Sloane, 1981; Taber, 1983).

Programs that allow the teacher to input content to individualize instruction for each child are a necessity. Several program "shells" of this type are commercially available (Kleinman & Humphrey, 1982), with some providing the additional option of synchronizing tape-recorded cues and/or stimulus presentations with the lesson (Hartley, 1983). These are generally very easy to operate, and require no programming skill on the part of the teacher. They are limited, however, in that the shells are designed to accept verbal or numerical input only (i.e., spelling words and math problems). For the teacher of nonreading students, who has to rely exclusively on graphic presentation of information, there are no comparable authoring packages in terms of simplicity of use. Resources are available to assist in creating lessons involving sound and graphics (e.g., various versions of Apple Pilot), but more time is required to learn the programming language.

Commercial software is currently available in several content areas relevant to career education. A review of educational computer catalogs (Hartley, 1983; MCE, 1983), for example, indicated that software has been developed for instruction in the areas of money concepts, time telling, calendar skills, word recognition, and home health and safety. Furthermore, a Job Readiness Assessment and Development Series, which branches to accommodate reading levels equivalent to grades 3 to 6, and a Job Survival Series, geared to the junior high to high school student, are new products available from MCE, Inc. (1983). Topics such as Job Readiness Attitude Assessment, Filling Out Job Applications, Successful Job Interviewing, and Resources for Job Hunting are included in these packages. However, it must be stressed that this software is designed for the nonhandicapped student.

Staff Development

Assuming that an adequate hardware/software combination has been found, the final consideration for a successful integration of micro-computer technology in training programs for the handicapped relates to the method of implementation. Teacher support and participation in the installation and implementation of microcomputers in classroom settings is critical. After completing a review of the literature regarding educational technology, Simmons (1975) wrote:

> Teachers are the key to any effective implementation of the technological media. Their opposition guarantees failure of even the best systems. Even if adoption of particular technological systems or projects must be postponed, educating teachers in the philosophy and implementation of technology is prerequisite to any successful implementation. No proposed project should be adapted and moved into the stage of implementation until the teachers whom it will affect have been educated to the point where they can contribute largely to the planning and implementation of the project (p. ix).

The extent and type of computer applications a program is planning will be a major determinant of the type of training needed. Ringle (1981) stressed that relevant applications, matching the users' current interests and needs, will enhance a person's willingness to learn, thus facilitating the acceptance of the computer as an aid rather than a threat.

IMPACT OF MICROCOMPUTERS ON CAREER EDUCATION

Microcomputers will influence career education for the handicapped in the areas of objectives, instruction, and data management. Projections have been made that by the end of the 1980s 75% of all employment will involve computers (Cain, 1983). Thus, computer literacy becomes an important new objective. Commack School District in New York has 6 years' experience in developing a K–12 computer literacy program for handicapped students. Their comprehensive and functional computer literacy program serves as a model for other districts to replicate (Cain, 1983). Another way that objectives are affected by computer technology is in the type and number of objectives that are specified. Microcomputer-based instruction can expand the range of objectives possible. For example, severely physically handicapped persons can control portions of their environment through voice command and recognition systems enabling them a degree of independence formerly not envisioned (Launey, 1981). Similarly, computer-based augmentative communication systems have significantly altered the content and fluency of cerebral palsied persons' communication patterns (Cohn, 1981).

Second, microcomputers can enhance instruction. By carefully pacing new information and varying the informational context the computer can increase the chances of retention and understanding of concepts. As noted earlier in this chapter, the capacity for individualizing and branching helps to produce errorless learning.

Finally, computers can serve important management information functions by collecting, storing, summarizing, and analyzing data in an ongoing fashion. Furthermore, lessons or tasks can be sequentially arranged according to each student's performance patterns. Timely data on student responses is critical for formative as well as summative evaluation purposes.

In summary, a renewed emphasis on career education programs for the handicapped is required. Special types of career education programs are recommended, programs that follow a functional curriculum conducted in normalized settings and that reflect the latest technologies. Appropriate and judicious selection of microcomputer systems can enable staff to address and possibly overcome the limitations of contemporary career education programs identified earlier in this chapter. The microcomputer can provide more relevant instruction to severely handicapped students and to younger students, as well as with their non-handicapped peers. Such programs will enable the handicapped to better fulfill their roles at work, in the home, and in the community.

REFERENCES

Allard, K., & Thorkildsen, R. (1981). Intelligent videodiscs for special education. *Videodisc News*, 2(4), 6–7.

Becker, R. L., Widener, Q., & Soforenko, A. Z. (1979). Career education for trainable mentally retarded youth. *Education and Training of the Mentally Retarded*, 14(2), 101–105.

Bellamy, G. T., Sheehan, M., Horner, R., & Boles, S. (1980). Community programs for severely handicapped adults: An analysis. *Journal of the Association for the Severely Handicapped*, 5, 307–324.

Bijou, S. W. (1970). What psychology has to offer education—Now. *Journal of Applied Behavior Analysis*, 5(1), 65–71.

Brickey, M., & Campbell, K. (1981). Fast food employment for moderately and mildly mentally retarded adults. *Mental Retardation*, 19, 113–116.

Brolin, D. E. (1977). Career development: A national priority. *Education and Training of the Mentally Retarded*, 12, 154–156.

Brolin, D. E. (Ed.). (1978). *Life-centered career education: A competency based approach*. Reston, VA: Council for Exceptional Children.

Brown, L., Falvey, M., Vincent, L., Kaye, N., Johnson, F., Ferrara-Parrish, P., & Gruenewald, L. (1980). Strategies for generating comprehensive, longitudinal, and chronological-age-appropriate individualized education programs for adolescent and young-adult severely handicapped students. *Journal of Special Education*, 14(2), 199–215.

Budke, W. W., Bettis, G. E., & Beasley, G. F. (1972). *Career education practice*. Columbus, OH: ERIC Clearinghouse on Vocational and Technical Education.

Bureau of Education for the Handicapped. (1975). *Proceedings of the Conference on Research Needs Related to the Career Education of the Handicapped*. Washington, DC: U.S. Office of Education.

Cain, E. J. (1983). *Expanding horizons—Current and future potentials of microcomputer technology for all handicapped*. Paper presented at the

National Conference on the Use of Microcomputers in Special Education, Hartford, Connecticut, March.

Clark, G. M. (1979). *Career education for the handicapped child in the elementary classroom.* Denver: Love Publishing Company.

Cohn, J. T. (1981). Microcomputer augmentative communication devices. In Proceedings of the Johns Hopkins First National Search for Applications of Personal Computing to Aid the Handicapped, October 31, Washington, DC. Los Alamitos, CA: IEEE Computer Society.

Cosky, M. J. (1980). *Computer-based instruction and cognitive styles: Do they make a difference?* Paper presented at the National Conference on Computer-Based Education, Bloomington, Minnesota, October. (ERIC Document Reproduction Service No. ED 201 299).

D'Alonzo, B. J. (1977). Trends and issues in career education for the mentally retarded. *Education and Training of the Mentally Retarded, 12*(2), 156–158.

Eisele, J. E. (1980). A case for computers in instruction. *Journal of Research and Development in Education, 14*(1), 1–8.

Flanagan, W. M., & Schoepke, J. M. (1978). *Lifelong learning and career development needs of the severely handicapped.* Columbia: University of Missouri–Columbia. (ERIC Document Reproduction Service No. ED 162 700).

Gagne, R. M., & Briggs, L. J. (1979). *Principles of instructional design.* New York: Holt, Rinehart & Winston.

Halloran, W. D. Handicapped persons: (1978). Who are they? *American Vocational Journal, 53*(1), 30–31.

Hannaford, A., & Sloane, E. (1981). Microcomputers: Powerful learning tools with proper programming. *Teaching Exceptional Children, 14*(2), 54–57.

Hartley, J. (1983). K–10 Educational Software for Apple II. Dimondale, MI: Hartley Courseware, Inc.

Jay, T. B. (1981). Computerphobia: What to do about it. *Educational Technology, 21*, 47–48.

Juhrs, P. (1982). Successful model of first community-based residential, vocational, and educational services for severely and profoundly affected autistic adults and adolescents. Paper presented at the Maryland Society for Autistic Adults and Children Conference, Bethesda, Maryland, November.

Kazdin, A. E. (1980). *Behavior modification in applied settings.* Homewood, IL: Dorsey Press.

Kleinman, G., & Humphrey, M. (1982). Writing your own software: Authoring tools make it easy. *Electronic Learning, May/June*, 36–41.

Kokaska, C. (1978). Career awareness for handicapped students in elementary schools. *Career Development for Exceptional Individuals, 1*, 25–35.

Launey, R. O. (1981). The motor-handicapped support system. In the Proceedings of the Johns Hopkins First National Search for Applications of Personal Computing to Aid the Handicapped, October 31, Washington, DC. Los Alamitos, CA: IEEE Computer Society.

Lawton, J., & Gerschner, V. T. (1982). A review of the literature on attitudes toward computers and computerized instruction. *Journal of Research and Development in Education, 16*(1), 50–55.

MCE—Microcomputer educational programs. (1983). Kalamazoo, MI: MCE Inc.

Mori, A. A. (1979). Vocational education and special education: A new partnership in career education. *Journal of Career Education, 6*(1), 55–67.

Reichle, J., Williams, W., Vogelsburg, T., and Williams, F. C. (1980). Curricula for the severely handicapped: Components and evaluation criteria. In B. Wilcox & R. York (Eds.), *Quality education for the severely handicapped.* Washington, DC: U.S. Department of Education.

Ringle, M. (1981). Computer literacy: New directions and new aspects. *Computers and People, November/December,* 12–15.

Rusch, F. R., & Mithaug, D. E. (1980). *Vocational training for mentally retarded adults.* Champaign, IL: Research Press.

Schwejda, P. & Vanderheiden, G. (1983). Adaptive-firmware card for the Apple II. *Byte, 7*(9), 276–314.

Simmons, L. N. (1975). Effects of educational technology: A review of the literature (Research Report No. IR76-800-71-14). Dallas Independent School District, Department of Research, Evaluation, and Information Systems, Dallas, Texas, November.

Snell, M. E. (Ed.). (1978). *Systematic instruction of the moderately and severely handicapped.* Columbus, OH: Charles E. Merrill.

Sowers, J., Thompson, L., & Connis, R. (1979). The food service vocational training program. In G. T. Bellamy, G. O'Connor, & O. C. Karan (Eds.), *Vocational rehabilitation of severely handicapped persons.* Baltimore: University Park Press.

Sprafkin, R. P., Gershaw, N. J., & Goldstein, A. P. (1978). Teaching interpersonal skills to psychiatric outpatients: Using structured learning therapy in a community-based setting. *Journal of Rehabilitation, 44*(2), 26–29.

Taber, F. M. (1983). *Microcomputers in special education.* Reston, VA: Council for Exceptional Children.

Tawney, J. W., & Cartwright, G. P. (1981). Teaching in a technology oriented society. *Teacher Education and Special Education, 4*(3), 3–14.

Tawney, J. W., Knapp, D. S., O'Reilly, C. D., & Pratt, S. S. (1979). *Programmed environments curriculum for the handicapped.* Columbus, OH: Charles E. Merrill.

U.S. Department of Health, Education, and Welfare, Office of Education, Office of Career Education. (1975). *An introduction to career education.* Washington, DC: Government Printing Office.

U.S. Department of Labor Employment Standards Administration. (1982). *A study of accommodations provided to handicapped employees by federal contractors.* Final Report. Berkeley, CA: Berkeley Planning Associates.

U.S. Federal Register, May 4, 1977, Volume *42*(86). (P.L. 93-112)

U.S. Federal Register, August 23, 1977, *42*(191). (P.L. 94-142).

U.S. Federal Register, October 3, 1977, *42*(191). (P.L. 94-482).

Walls, R. T., Zane, T., & Werner, T. J. (1979). *The vocational behavioral checklist.* Dunbar, WV: West Virginia Research and Training Center.

Wehman, P., Hill, M., Goodall, P., Cleveland, P., Brooke, V., & Pentecost, J. H. (1982). Job placement and follow-up of moderately and severely handicapped individuals after three years. *Journal of the Association for the Severely Handicapped, 7*(2), 5–16.

Wehman, P., Hill, J., & Koehler, F. (1979). Helping severely handicapped persons enter competitive employment. *Journal of the Association for the Severely Handicapped, 4,* 274–290.

Wilcox, B., & Bellamy, G. T. (1982). *Design of high school programs for severely handicapped students.* Baltimore: Paul H. Brookes.

5

The Physically Handicapped and Career Development

Donald R. Rabush

Jules Feiffer has a cartoon that I think captures the concept of career development. The caption reads:

> When I was a kid—I used to dream of what I wanted to be as a grownup—a test pilot—a cowboy—a ball player. Now I'm forty. And I'm not a test pilot; I'm not a cowboy; I'm not a ball player; and I'm not a grownup. Who ever dreamed it would be this hard?

"Becoming" is difficult under normal circumstances; it surely is much more difficult for those who are physically handicapped.

The population that is circumscribed under the rubric of physically handicapped is a very diverse one. It includes, among others, those who are blind, partially sighted, deaf, hard of hearing, or have cerebral palsy, spina bifida, or other orthopedic and health impairments. These handicaps and some major problems, including myths and traditions, that affect career guidance are discussed briefly.

VISUAL IMPAIRMENTS

Visually impaired is a generic term that refers to individuals who have problems with vision. Legal and educational definitions are helpful in the discussion of the degree of visual loss and its impact. Based on acuity, the term *legally blind* is defined as a person whose vision is no better than 20/200 after correction or whose visual field subtends to an angle of 20 degrees or less. Only a very small percentage of the visually impaired population is totally blind or without any usable sight. A partially sighted child is one who can be educated using visual materials. A blind child, on the other hand, is one whose visual loss indicates that he or she would be best served using braille, tactile, and auditory materials.

The extent of the visual impairment is a major factor that must be considered in the career development process. How should career material be delivered? What is the best format? What occupations are most suitable? What careers should be excluded? With the advancement in technology, the extent of the impairment may not pose the same problem in career selection that it used to. The Optacon converts print into tactile vibrations; the Kurzweil Reading Machine reads books and other printed material aloud using synthetic speech; voice output devices complement the computer. These and many other exciting advances in technology help bridge the gap for many of the visually impaired who wish to enter into the visual world of work.

A larger problem associated with severity of vision loss is how the parents of the visually impaired individual cope with the problem early in the child's life. Many parents of young visually impaired children bring negative feelings and prejudices to the early interactions with their handicapped child. The word "blind" conjures up a number of less-than-positive images: the person with the tin cup, the helpless person stumbling around. Sayings such as "down a blind alley," "blind chance," and "blind fury" surely cannot be considered positive. These may well be the initial thoughts that parents have when they learn that their child is visually impaired.

Considering the high probability that parents bring some learned prejudices to the interaction with their visually impaired child, it is not surprising that many negative feelings are transmitted. Imamura (1965) concluded that it is not so much the lack of sight itself, but the differential social treatment that the visually impaired receive from others that make them more or less dependent as individuals. Scott (1969), in *The Making of Blind Men*, succinctly stated that self-concept is not something a person is born with, but a product of socialization. Visually impaired children learn to see themselves and respond to the world as their parents and siblings, the most significant others early in their lives, responded to them.

Early decisions that parents make regarding the child's handicap may have a profound effect on career choice and availability. The decision-making continuum might follow this pattern:

1. Early decisions about explorations may affect mobility.
2. Mobility surely will affect independence or dependence.

3. Independence or dependence may affect assertiveness or passiveness.
4. Passive behavior may foster overprotection.
5. Overprotection may limit experiences.
6. Limited experiences will color judgment.
7. Poor judgments may be labeled as immaturity, which surely will affect the way the environment positively or negatively reinforces the individual.

This is just one example of how early interaction can have a long-term detrimental effect.

Another crucial early decision is schooling: public versus private, day versus residential. This placement will surely determine the amount and type of career development activities to which the child is exposed. Unfortunately, parents need to make the schooling decision early, often without the full understanding of the ramifications of that decision. In the past, residential schools for the visually impaired were reasonably large facilities that had both academic and vocational programs with a wide range of career options. The dramatic decline in the number of blind individuals, primarily due to medical advancements, has changed these institutions and they are now serving a larger percentage of multiply handicapped individuals. The expertise for educational intervention and career development is still there, but the population has changed. Urban centers also may have reasonable programming, but less populated communities are unable to provide a full complement of services, in terms of both academic programming and career development.

HEARING IMPAIRMENT

Heward and Orlansky (1980) stated that there is no legal definition of the "hearing-impaired" population. Like all handicapping conditions, we have gradations of the problem along a continuum. The range, or degree of loss, is from normal through hard of hearing to deafness. A second variable is age of onset (i e., whether a person is born with the problem or whether he or she acquires the hearing loss after the onset of language). The final variable is whether the hearing loss is conductive or sensorineural. We list the above variables to suggest to the reader that this population itself is very diverse and that one must understand all the variables that affect the functioning of a person with a hearing loss.

If we look briefly only at the degree of loss, we can group the population into two major clusters. First, those whose loss is from 25 dB through approximately 70 dB are considered to have a slight, mild, or marked hearing loss. This group is reasonably successful with traditional speech and language training and, given good auditory training, can function as would a hearing group. This population most probably will receive academic training in the mainstream of public education. They may have some problem in language development, which may affect reading ability and, therefore, academic performance. Individuals with marked loss may, in addition, have some social development problems, but for general practice they are more similar to their hearing peers than dissimilar. The second cluster, those with severe and profound hearing losses, need specialized educational programming and are probably most appropriately served educationally in a self-contained or residential program. These individuals have language-related problems and must rely on vision rather than hearing as their primary avenue for communication (Heward & Orlansky, 1980).

There are two important facts to remember about the severe and profound hearing loss population. First, the vast majority of deaf/hard-of-hearing youngsters have hearing parents who want their children to be as normal as possible. Second, this is a language-based problem that has major ramifications on the quantity and quality of language developed. Obviously this handicap creates an auditory deficit; in many cases, it requires an alternate form of receptive and expressive language (viz., sign language). Knowledge of these facts helps us understand that the parents of hearing-impaired children will have problems interacting with them from the onset of the hearing loss.

Because language learning normally occurs during early childhood through the parent/environment interaction with the child, we have a disfunctional learning pattern right from the start. Communication is also crucial in the interaction between parent and child and in all social contact with the environment. For all of these reasons, the hearing-impaired population is highly susceptible to language problems, not just speech or expressive language problems, but also receptive language problems, communication problems, and, ultimately, academic problems. Poor academic achievement in this population often results in problems in self-concept development. Telford and Sawrey (1981) stated that the barriers of hearing loss certainly increase the total incidence of frustration, loneliness, helplessness, and despair. Others note that, like most other handicapped groups, the hearing impaired display a greater than normal tendency to limit their levels of aspiration in the interest of avoiding failure rather than striving for the approval of high achievement (Stinson, 1974). Thus, although causes of hearing loss may differ, the exhibited behavior has the same profound effect on the career development process.

Individuals with slight and mild losses will probably obtain career information with their hearing peers and require very little adaptation of career information or career goals. The individuals with marked loss may need more adaptations depending on their oral skills. If the oral skills are minimally developed they may demonstrate an inability to comfortably fit into either the hearing or the deaf culture. If these individuals receive career information in the public school setting, it may not be appropriate to their needs.

Traditionally, the deaf have worked in many trades associated with printing. This obviously was because the deaf were not bothered by the volume of noise associated with presses and other equipment. Even so, this is a stereotypical placement and, with the move to computer typesetting, is especially inappropriate as a self-fulfilling prophecy in the 1980s. The typical deaf student is educated in a residential school program where a variety of career options of a vocational nature are offered. Here, a good exposure to deaf adult role models and a good awareness of the world of work is provided.

PHYSICAL AND HEALTH IMPAIRMENTS

The physically and health-impaired population is another very diverse group. The most common impairment in this population is cerebral palsy, a nonprogressive motor or posture disorder that is caused by a malfunction of or damage to the brain. The most frequent types of motor problems associated with cerebral palsy are spasticity (severe muscle tension), athetosis (slow, writhing movements), and ataxia (coordination and balance problems). The most important information to understand about cerebral palsy is that it is nonprogressive and that it is congenital in approximately 85% of cases. There are, of course, varying degrees of severity and there is a higher degree of mental retardation associated with cerebral palsy than with the normal population.

Spina bifida is the second most common physical handicap. This condition is due to abnormal fetal development. There are three different forms of the disorder, which vary in severity. Bleck and Nagel (1982) stated that myelomeningocele (one form of spina bifida) presents an almost overwhelming series of disabilities. Because of the need for much medical intervention, there is usually a great amount of school time lost. This type of child may have reduced academic performance, not because of intellectual inability but because of undeveloped skills. Because decreased mobility is the primary manifestation of the handicap, elementary school-age children should, for the most part, be prepared for sedentary vocations, trade schools, high school, and college, according to Bleck and Nagel (1982).

The physical aspects and demands of many career options are the major problems associated with orthopedically limited children. Bleck and Nagel (1982) stated that these children are often more capable than society allows or expects. It is important that counselors and career specialists do not underestimate the potential of this population. This is no easy task because many of these clients perceive themselves as having limited capabilities. Harper and Richman (1978), investigating the personality profile of the orthopedically disabled, found that generally this population is behaviorally inhibited and exhibits a sense of isolation, a passive orientation to interpersonal interaction, and a generalized feeling of alienation. Surely these types of personal projections affect counselor perceptions.

For discussion of numerous other orthopedic problems, the reader is referred to *Physically Handicapped Children: A Medical Atlas for Teachers*, by Bleck and Nagel (1982).

The major problems in health impairment that the career specialist needs to understand are epilepsy, a convulsive disorder that is usually controlled with medication; diabetes, a metabolic disorder treatable with medication; and asthma, a respiratory problem. Most of the health impairments are well explained and controlled by the medical community and are also explained by Bleck and Nagel (1982). There are, however, a number of psychological problems in both populations that are associated with the physical symptoms that affect career choice.

Sirvis, Carpignano, and Bigge (1977) suggested the following possible problems:

1. Unresolved dependence feelings
2. Excessive submissiveness
3. Extreme egocentrism
4. Fantasy as a compensation for inferiority feelings
5. Resignation to rather than recognition of limits
6. A superficial conscious recognition of the handicap with a subconscious rejection of self

This surely is a difficult group of individuals for the career specialist to deal with. In most cases the career development information is provided in the mainstream setting and the information provider has limited information on how to adapt career goals. Sirvis et al. (1977) suggested that some factors to consider are personal strength and stamina, mobility, toileting problems, communication skills, and potential for skill development. Of course an understanding of the medical condition and its ramifications is also crucial.

THE DISABILITY AND CAREER DEVELOPMENT

Each handicapped child by virtue of his or her disability poses a very unique set of problems for parents and educators. Suran and Rizzo (1979) stated that it is virtually impossible to include all physically handicapped children under a single set of descriptive terms. Because of their disabilities and/or illnesses, physically impaired and health-impaired children may require modification in communication, in their physical environment, in instruction, and in other aspects of an education program. There are also numerous variables that impinge on the developing individual that create personal adjustment problems.

There is a preponderance of evidence that indicates that parents of disabled students go through various states of acceptance of the child and his or her disability. In this process they deal with denial, search for a cure, anger, and so forth. This process may take 5, 10, or 20 years; in fact, for some individuals the process may never end. This may account for some problems in self-concept development. There are numerous variables that affect the development of self-concept and the emotional adjustment of physically handicapped individuals. Concepts such as acceptance, belonging, sexual development, and economic security are all part of this self-adjustment. Because many of the career guidance theories and materials focus on self-concept and self-perception, the career development assumptions that are used in the able-bodied community become somewhat unstable when applied to this population. For example, Herr and Cramer (1979) have suggested that career guidance be broken into awareness and accommodation in the elementary school. They listed the following subgoals as important.

Awareness (K–3)

1. Awareness of self
2. Awareness of different types of occupational roles
3. Awareness of individual's responsibility for own actions
4. Development of the rudiments of classification and decision-making skills
5. Learning cooperative social behavior
6. Development of respect for others and the work that they do

Accommodation (4–6)

1. Development of concepts related to self
2. Development of concepts related to the world of work
3. Assuming increased responsibility for planning one's time

4. Application of decision-making and classification skills
5. Development of desirable social relationships
6. Development of work attitudes and values

The very first goals in awareness and accommodation deal with self-concept and how one's future career goals hinge on the perception of the mesh between the world of work and one's personal needs and desires. For many disabled individuals the whole process of acceptance of one's own handicap is much more basic and is crucial before one can move to the accommodation process. All of this is tied to the early acceptance of the handicap by the parents.

The problem with the diversity of this population regarding acceptance is that the whole career guidance process may well be disfunctional because of the following factors:

1. Disabled individuals may not have a reasonable self-concept or any idea of how their needs and assets interface with career options.
2. The quality and quantity of career services vary dramatically by virtue of the educational setting in which the individuals find themselves and by the definition of career education that the different systems subscribe to.
3. Disabled persons may not have any disabled adult role models or an understanding of what career options may be available.
4. The counselor or deliverer of service may harbor biases that shape the information offered and thus develop a skewed picture of opportunities.
5. We live in a world that is resistant to hiring disabled persons. Last hired, first fired is too often the axiom associated with this group by some employers.

THE DELIVERY OF SERVICE

Since the inception of P.L. 94-142 (the Education for All Handicapped Children Act), an increasing number of physically handicapped students are being educated "in the mainstream," which, translated, means in public schools. Before this, some students were placed in segregated day schools or residential schools or given home and hospital instruction. The public education environment is where the majority of career guidance occurs. There are also vocational rehabilitation centers that provide career services for individuals who are beyond school age. Although the intent of mainstreaming is to provide equal education in terms of cognitive education, when it comes to fulfilling career expectations, a very unequal situation exists.

In the public school setting career development needs of disabled youth have, to date, been subsumed largely within the general career education efforts and consequently have not received any special attention. There are also problems of counselor prejudices, which may affect what career material is offered and under what conditions, and a lack of role models or realistic career expectations. In residential schools there may be fewer prejudices, more role models, and more realistic career expectations, but there also is much more emphasis on vocational training as opposed to career guidance. Finally, the rehabilitation center provides more direct vocational instruction than broad career assistance. There has been very little concentrated effort on the part of those of us in the field of career education, who are supposed to be concerning ourselves with the career development opportunities of *all* youth, to meet the special needs of these "special" children. Consequently, these students have had to rely on luck with respect to career planning and development. Regrettably, luck is not working for the vast majority (Moffit, 1978).

There has been limited training of teachers and counselors about handicapping conditions and their impact on career perspectives for this population. Specialized materials—although somewhat available—are not in the classrooms where instruction is taking place. Carolyn Raymond (1978), Director of Career Development in Mesa, Arizona, asked "Are we really interested in the career development of the disabled?" For several individuals across the nation the answer has been "yes" for a number of years. For the vast majority of educators, however, the response has been one of passive resistance. While special educational programs for these individuals have increased and improved in general curriculum areas within our schools, little, if any, special effort has been made to address their career development needs. There are some notable exceptions: Brolin in *Life Centered Career Education: A Competency-based Approach* (1978) provided suggestions for teachers of special populations and Cegelka in her chapter on Career Education in *An Introduction to Special Education* (1981) proposed that the best way to deliver career information to this population is either through infusion or separate programming; she also provided some good suggestions for implementation. The theory is in place; in actual practice, however, we see a great variety in delivery due to the commitment and training of the teacher and the location of the service.

Those students who receive their educational training in residential programs seem to be obtaining career education from another perspective. In most cases career expectations are more realistic, neither over- nor underestimating the students because of their physical handicap. These programs tend to be more vocationally oriented than their public school counterparts. In public school settings many physically handicapped students are excluded from participation in vocational programs, even though the Vocational Education Act of 1973 guarantees access to this population. In 1978, Hoyt defined career education as a broader concept than paid employment and vocational skills. He went on to say that in these times of rapid societal and occupational change, education as preparation for work can no longer be limited in meaning to the acquisition of specific vocational skills needed for entry into the occupational society. Instead, he insisted, it must include providing students with adaptability skills, basic academic skills, effective work habits, a personally meaningful set of work values, career decision-making skills, and job-seeking, job-getting and job-holding skills. Educators must become as concerned about helping graduates get along and move up in the world of paid employment as they are with helping them gain initial entry into that world. Thus, we have added the concept of mastering adaptability skills to the goals of vocational education, as well as preparation for specific work.

Unfortunately, residential programs find themselves years behind. They have developed reasonably large vocational training facilities that have served as the focus of their career programs for the past decade. With the availability of federal dollars in the early 1970s, many vocational programs flourished in these schools. In 1973, the New Jersey School for the Deaf reported 26 different areas of vocational training available to its students. Today there are some 30 programs in addition to a large vocational assessment program. Rapid technological change, which has altered the face of vocational programming, makes it difficult for schools to keep their vocational offerings synchronized with the skills needed by business and industry. Along with the shrinking of federal dollars and the diminishing size and changing nature of the student population, schools have been forced to broaden their vocational programming into more general career training using career clusters rather than occupational skills specialties. This leaves more specialized technical occupational training to postsecondary schools and challenges the secondary school and their middle and lower school components to rethink and revise their entire career curriculum.

Most of the residential programs that serve the physically handicapped have no formalized career education program. A recent interview with Jan Neidermaier (personal communication, Trenton, NJ, January 27, 1982), one of two career counselors in secondary residential schools for the deaf on the Eastern seaboard, indicated that their approach would be one that would infuse material into the total school curriculum. She was having considerable difficulty finding suitable material for the deaf population because of language level difficulty. Even in the general area of decision making, for instance, adequate materials are not available. Thus, her job has become one of "cutting and pasting" from many sources to develop a minimal career program. One can only guess what is occurring in other programs where no person is responsible for career education. As Hoyt (1978) so aptly stated, the promise of career education remains much more evident than does its effective delivery.

There are rehabilitation centers available for those individuals who, for one reason or another, approach the world of work without specific career goals or for the individual who becomes adventitiously physically handicapped. A phone survey of five major rehabilitation centers in Maryland, Virginia, Pennsylvania, New Jersey, and New York indicated that they are directed toward training programs with career guidance as an overlay. This career aspect deals with such major thrusts as:

1. Entering into job training programs
2. Work or personal adjustment programs
3. Long-term sheltered workshops
4. Direct job placement

If this, then, is the current status of career education for the physically handicapped, what have been the results in the real world as measured by inclusion of the handicapped into the world of work? Surely it is obvious that the past decade has seen a positive change in the attitude toward all handicapped persons. P.L. 94-142, Section 504 of the Vocational Rehabilitation Act of 1973, with its increased media coverage, and the International Year of the Disabled have all contributed to a higher visibility. Yet the bottom line is still an inability for the physically handicapped to obtain and retain employment. We also find an extra-ordinarily high rate of underemployment. An example makes this reality perfectly clear. In 1976, a young woman entered the Western Maryland College graduate program in special education. After attending full-time, she graduated with close to an A average in 1978, fully certified to teach special education children. This woman, in her twenties, has cerebral palsy, is confined to a wheelchair, and has some speech disarticulation. She is a bright, black female, with 33 hours beyond her master's degree, and still does not have a full-time job. She was a clerk for the federal government and now is a substitute teacher.

Hoyt (1979), in his monograph "Career Education and the Handicapped Person," indicated that of the approximately 2.5 million handicapped youths who will leave our school systems in the next 4 years only 21% will be either fully employed or enrolled in college; more than one million, or 40% will be underemployed and at the poverty level, 8% will be in their home community and idle much of the time, 25% will be unemployed and on welfare, and 3% will be totally dependent and institutionalized. Davidson (1981) stated that if the recession has thrown millions of Americans out of work, no group is having a tougher time in the tight job market than disabled persons. While the jobless rate fluctuates around 10%, about one-half of the 15 million disabled citizens cannot find jobs. Why is 50% of the disabled population currently unemployed? We certainly can question our current preparation systems. We need to look forward to positive options that are available to those of us who possibly can make things happen.

FOCUSING ON POSITIVE CHANGE

A successful career education program for disabled individuals belongs to more than just the disabled themselves. All segments of society need to be in a sense "desensitized" with respect to physical and sensory handicaps. We must reach the point that we can look a disabled person directly in the eye, recognize and admit his or her disability, and then accept that person for what she or he can, rather than cannot, do (Hoyt, 1978).

We must spend more time addressing the attitudes of the general population, and especially those of potential employers. Many employers are reluctant to make jobs available to the disabled because they fear that they will have to make expensive modifications at the workplace. In addition, employers are concerned with lost time on the job. Even though these stereotypes are without factual basis, they prevail. Furthermore, general prejudices about the deaf, blind, and physically handicapped are prevalent in all strata in our society, and in the field of special education as well as across academia. General attitude change will occur if we persist faithfully, but our efforts need to be revitalized and continued or all of the career education in the world will be of no real benefit.

Teacher training, both preservice and inservice, must be altered. Those of us who are responsible for developing teacher training programs at the college and university level dealing with the physically handicapped must begin to devote more time to career education. Informal surveys the author conducted with teachers in 1979 and recently indicated that they were being prepared for their classroom role with little or no knowledge of or appreciation for career education. They do not understand the career development process or the special relevance that career education must have in the school experience. As Herr has observed elsewhere, this is probably true of preservice programs throughout the United States.

In-service training for teachers and counselors who are already in the field is an obvious need. First, we must help the regular classroom teacher deal with the acceptance of the disabled. Research has proven that the teacher's attitude toward the handicap is the single most crucial variable in the acceptance of the disabled child within the school setting. If we are to make an impact on future generations, we must begin attitude training in the schools today. For the last 4 years we have been running a mainstreaming project for middle school teachers and students at Western Maryland College. We have provided approximately 500 teachers and 7,500 students with some 40 different experiences in almost 100 hours of training and contact with disabled persons and have made measurable changes in attitudes. This type of in-depth in-service training is mandatory if teachers in the public schools are going to teach the physically handicapped. Without this training, teachers may instill their biases, inevitably influencing the child's self-concept and confidence, which may cause extremely negative effects. Furthermore, these same teachers need quality information about career education for all students if we are going to attempt to infuse career material throughout the K–12 curriculum. All of this is more critical when applied to the school counselor, who will be more directly involved in providing leadership both for the inclusion of "special students" and the infusion of career education. It has been observed that in individual counseling, for example, trained and presumably sensitive counselors often shun mention of a physical disability or pretend that "it" does not matter to goals. If this is being done to the physically handicapped by those who would be directing the program, surely we can understand the need for improved training. The Maryland State Department of Education Divisions of Special Education and Pupil Services offered two statewide conferences in 1981 on handicapped awareness. They predicted that by 1985 every teacher and counselor will have had one course dealing with general information about handicapped children. This certainly is a positive step, but why not infuse special adaptations regarding career education in those training hours? Then the training might be translated into more realistic career goals for future beneficiaries.

Concurrent with such training components should be the development of materials in resource centers where teachers and students alike can go to obtain career education information. In November of 1979, the National Technical Institute for the Deaf compiled an annotated bibliography entitled, "Career Education: A Bibliography of Research Studies and Programs for Handicapped Americans." More up-to-date efforts of this nature need to be suggested, supported, and disseminated.

THE COMPUTER, CAREER GUIDANCE, AND THE PHYSICALLY HANDICAPPED

One tool that has unlimited value to this population is the computer. The computer can be used for environmental control, entertainment, educational or occupational fulfillment, and career guidance. For each of the outlined populations peripheral devices, hardware, or interface items have been developed that make access to all programs possible.

Recent articles in popular computer magazines indicate how important the computer can be to the physically handicapped. Auslander (1983), the father of a 15-year-old deaf child, wrote:

> Undoubtedly the greatest benefit Lisa has gotten from this computer has been communicating with other computer enthusiasts who are on the Bulletin Board System (BBS). Access to various computer information services such as Compu-Serve and the Source has helped her improve her hearing and language skills. In our home, the computer has become a sound track to the world.

Another article, "Computers Help Non-verbal Patients to Speak" appeared in *Personal Computing* (January, 1983).

> Edgar is a 21-year-old cerebral palsy victim who also suffers from dyslexia. Like many other patients using the computer in the Augmentative Devices program at Goldwater Memorial, Edgar is non-vocal, which means he has lost the ability to speak. Although cerebral palsy severely hampers his coordination, Edgar can type words and sentences into the terminal of his Apple computer. The computer automatically corrects misspelled words, allowing Edgar to communicate with others more effectively. His messages can either be printed out, or processed through a Votrax speech synthesizer, which sounds out the words in English.

It is becoming easier to find articles in rehabilitation literature that demonstrate the many ways the computer can be used by the physically handicapped. In addition to this, workshops and courses are being offered across the United States to teach how the computer can be harnessed to meet the specific needs of the disabled. One such conference, Computers for the Disabled, held in September 1983 at the University of Wisconsin-Stout reflected the state of the art at that time. Their brochure stated:

> The advent of microcomputers has provided a new and potentially powerful tool for the disabled and those working with them. The purpose of this conference is to provide an overview of the many areas in which computers can serve the needs of the disabled and some specific applications of this new medium.

The workshops included:

A. DEAF AND HEARING IMPAIRED   The microcomputer and language; what software to use and why; new tools bring new paths to written language development; telecommunications; talking to the rest of the world by microcomputers

B. BLIND AND VISION IMPAIRED   New technology and new tools; speech synthesis and low-cost automated Grade II braille;

visual simulation through the microcomputer; programs for braille training; what software and hardware does the job;

C. PHYSICALLY HANDICAPPED Everyone can have access to the microcomputer; hardware and software modifications; single switch interaction; voice entry systems; communication and environmental control

The hardware is available today; however, specialized software is another story. Most individuals adapt regular software to help meet the special needs of the handicapped. Unfortunately, in the area of career guidance this has not happened on a national basis. The six major computerized guidance programs that are described in Chapter 7 of this text need to be supplemented by the following two additions:

CHOICES (Computerized Heuristic Occupational Information and Career Exploration System) (based in Canada), used in employment offices, some high schools, community colleges, and universities

COIN (Coordinated Occupational Information Network), used in secondary schools, CETA, vocational rehabilitation, and others

None of those mentioned in this text have been adapted for the handicapped, however. Only three have been used in vocational rehabilitation settings—COIN, CIS (Career Information System), and GIS (Guidance Information System)—and then only on a very limited basis. The major access problem in terms of immediate use of these programs is the reading level. The CVIS (Computerized Vocational Information System) program, at sixth grade readability, appears to be the easiest to read. Others are directed at the high school level (Clyde, 1979).

CVIS is currently exploring the possibility of adapting its system for the handicapped. A concept paper prepared by the consortium stated:

> With the development of P.L. 94-142 and the whole concept of mainstreaming, larger numbers of handicapped individuals are being served by public school counselors. Training programs which deal with career counseling for the handicapped are nonexistent. Therefore, each counselor relies on his/her own knowledge of and experience with occupational opportunities for the handicapped. In most cases, this knowledge is very limited. At the present time there are very few resources available for counselors who are doing career counseling with handicapped individuals. In contrast, the resources available for career counseling for the wider population are voluminous and varied. Recent advances in technology have moved this field into the computer age, with a number of career guidance products being programmed for use on computers, both large mainframes and microcomputers. Most of these computer-based career guidance systems provide in-depth information about the broad spectrum of occupations which make up the world of work, discussing such topics as work tasks, work setting, personal requirements, educational training, salary and demand, and

others. None of these systems deal with job opportunities for individuals with handicaps. (Rabush, 1982)

This type of system, with an adapted data base and a reduced readability, would be a major step forward for both the physically handicapped and the field of career guidance. It is hoped that other major systems will also consider adjusting their programs in comparable ways.

CONCLUSIONS

1. The physically handicapped are a very diverse population. Each of the separate conditions represents a host of variables that create thousands of individuals who are very different from one another.
2. Because of the personal differences of each individual and the difference between parental expectation and the child's limitations there are problems of acceptance. These problems frequently are transmitted to the handicapped individuals, often resulting in low self-esteem. Since career guidance is hinged on self-concept, there is reason to believe that we need to place special emphasis on self-concept development with the physically handicapped, or their perceptions of the world of work may be limited by historically diminished expectations of society.
3. The professionals—educators, counselors, and administrators who work in the mainstream—are not prepared to assist this population in meeting their potential. These professionals have acquired biased attitudes and therefore limit the horizons of their students by offering biased information and a skewed view of the students' place in the working world.
4. Schools are the major sources of career guidance, and vocational rehabilitation is a supplementary provider. If a physically handicapped student is in a mainstream school, he or she will receive the regular career guidance curriculum and little vocational training. In a residential school, more vocational programs are available and career guidance is more specifically designed for the handicapped. Vocational rehabilitation is particularly related to job-specific training with career guidance limited to specific individuals.
5. Both preservice and inservice training in career education need to be strengthened. Very few programs in special education include a career component.
6. Computer technology is available to ameliorate many physical problems for this population. Students/clients have access to the computer to run all kinds of software and course ware. They are

getting training in running programs and in maintaining the machines.

7. No nationwide computerized guidance and information career program has yet been developed for or tailored to this population.

If we are going to make career education available to the physically handicapped, we need to pay attention to their unique needs. We must convince all those who are concerned that the world of compensatory or "special" education can no longer be divorced from the world of work.

REFERENCES

Auslander, R. (1983). Computers for the hearing impaired. *Classroom Computer News*, *70*, March.

Bleck, E., & Nagel, D. (1982). *Physically handicapped children: A medical atlas for teachers* (2nd ed.). New York: Grune & Stratton.

Brolin, D. E. (1978). *Life centered career education: A Competency-based approach*. Reston, VA: Council for Exceptional Children.

Cegelka, P. T. (1981). Career Education. In A. Blackhurst & W. Berdine (Eds.), *An introduction to special education*. Boston: Little, Brown.

Clyde, J. (1979). *Computerized career information and guidance systems*. Information Series No. 178: The Eric Clearinghouse.

Computers for the disabled (brochure). Office of Continuing Education, University of Wisconsin-Stout, Summer, 1983.

Computers help non-verbal patients to speak. (1983). *Personal Computing*, *January*, 24–26.

Davidson, J. (1981). For disabled, jobs few—But many make it. *U.S. News and World Report*, *89*, 45.

Harper, D., & Richman, L. (1978). Personality profiles of physically impaired adolescents. *Journal of Clinical Psychology*, *34*, 636–642.

Herr, E., & Cramer, S. (1979). *Career guidance through the life span: Systematic approaches*, Boston: Little, Brown.

Heward, W., & Orlansky, M. (1980). *Exceptional children*. Columbus, OH: Charles E. Merrill.

Hoyt, K. B. (1977). *Refining the career education concept: Part II* (Monographs on Career Education). Washington, DC: U.S. Government Printing Office.

Hoyt, K. B. (1978). *Obstacles and opportunities in career education*. Washington, DC: U.S. Government Printing Office.

Hoyt, K. B. (1979). *Career education and the handicapped person* (Monograph). Washington, DC: U.S. Government Printing Office.

Imamura, S. (1965). *Mother and blind child*. New York: American Foundation for the Blind (Research Series No. 14).

Moffit, R. (1978). *It's what you can do that counts* (Training Module). Mesa, AZ: Public Schools.

National Technical Institute for the Deaf. (1979). *Career education: A bibliography of research studies and programs for handicapped Americans*. Rochester: Author.

Rabush, C. (1982). Career education and the handicapped: CVIS (a concept paper) (Monograph). CVIS Consortium. Rockford, Illinois.

Raymond, C. D. (1978). Where the action is! Implementing career education for the disabled through in-service training (Monograph). Second National Working Conference of Career Development, Washington, DC, September.

Scott, R. A. (1969). *The making of blind men: A study of adult socialization.* New York: Russell Sage Foundation.

Sirvis, B., Carpignano, J., & Bigge, J. L. (1977). Psychosocial Aspects of Physical Disabilities. In J. L. Bigge (ed.), *Teaching individuals with physical and multiple disabilities.* Columbus, OH: Charles E. Merrill.

Stinson, M. S. (1974). Relations between maternal reinforcement and help and the achievement motive in normal-hearing and hearing-impaired sons. *Developmental Psychology*, *3*(10), 348–353.

Suran, B. G., & Rizzo, J. V. (1979). *Special children: An integrative approach.* Glenview, IL: Scott, Foresman.

Telford, C. W., & Sawrey, J. M. (1981). *The exceptional individual* (4th ed.). Englewood Cliffs, NJ: Prentice-Hall.

6

The Computer's Role in Enhancing Career Development

Joann Harris-Bowlsbey

Before beginning to define and describe the computer's role in assisting individuals in the career development process, it seems appropriate to build some rationale for the use of this powerful technological tool in human services delivery, particularly in the delivery of services to special populations. The fields of guidance and special education have placed very high value on individualized personal attention to students and clients. Effectiveness in providing instruction and services has been positively related in theory and research to the transmission of positive regard, empathy, and acceptance to the student or client. Given this fact, what is the rationale for use of technology with our special populations and with our very special content?

Rationale for Use of Technology in Career Guidance

One of the most powerful reasons for use of technology is the tremendous motivational appeal it has, especially with today's adolescents and children. One of the major vendors of microprocessors has adopted a marketing strategy that exposes elementary school children to the use of their machines. Like the children who begged their parents in the early 1950s to get a television set, many of today's children are begging their parents to purchase a microcomputer for the home. One of the major vendors of microcomputers now markets its computers in Sears stores and cataloges; when software is available for the machine, it will also be marketed through the catalogue. For better or for worse, our younger generation is a generation addicted to television. The transition to learning from a TV set cabled to a microcomputer either at home or at school is an easy one. The addition of a videodisc player to that set of hardware, thus adding unlimited capability to use graphics, color, sound, and motion in conjunction with a microcomputer, will increase the present high level of appeal.

Several studies have documented the fact that secondary-level students would select the computer as a preferred mode of delivery of guidance and information. Although I cannot cite any formal documentation of this high appeal at the elementary or adult level, some trends in this direction are very evident. Observe any elementary classroom in which students are learning by computer and you will see good behavior, rapt attention, and high motivation. Adults are a mixed lot. Some have a high level of skepticism and some a fear of computer technology, and many of these adults are in the field of education. The use of computers is foreign to any experience or training in their past. Others are "freaked out" by the technology. On the other hand, witness the large number of clubs of adults who use, develop and share computer software. Witness also the increasing number of adults who are purchasing microcomputers for use in the home and the increasing number of microcomputers that are being given as gifts.

This reason for utilizing the computer for career guidance, then, is built on the appeal of present technology and the ever-increasing forward rush of the microcomputer revolution, one that will impact American life even more than the Industrial Revolution. Given this societal environment, why not capitalize on it to accomplish desirable end goals for career guidance and development?

A powerful second reason for using the computer for career guidance relates to the inherent capabilities of the machine itself and its associated devices. Some of those capabilities far exceed those of humans. Here are some examples. A microcomputer costing $3,000 to $6,000, weighing 60 to 80 pounds, and measuring $24'' \times 30''$, has the power to store and manipulate files that only a few years ago required an unmovable, very large mainframe costing $25,000 to $50,000. Such a microcomputer can now utilize 8-inch floppy disks, which hold a million characters of data, or varying sizes of small hard disks, which store up to 60 million characters of data. With this kind of power and storage, the present-day computer can instantaneously recall information about thousands of occupations, schools, jobs, or financial aids in nanoseconds—and that is one of its simpler tasks. The computer is capable of searching large files by a combination of variables selected by the user in order to provide assistance both in identifying the many options available and in narrowing those options in meaningful ways. Imagine the student who wants to identify occupations that require working with conceptual thinking, have a bright employment outlook, have potential to earn more than $30,000, do not require more than 2 years of education or training for entry, and allow some amount of travel as a part of the work tasks. Or imagine the deaf student who wants to find a 4-year college in the Northeast that has a major in computer science, costs less than $4000 per year, has at least a 10% black enrollment, provides interpreter service, has high potential for awarding financial aid, and accepts students with a mean SAT score of 500. These would be difficult searches for a human to perform even with the best of reference books, microfiche, and paper filing systems. Computers, however, are capable of storing, retrieving, and searching large files more quickly and efficiently than human beings.

There are other functions that the computer does very well. It does not mind working 18 to 24 hours per day in any kind of work setting—libraries, dorms, career guidance and development offices, personnel offices, prisons, shopping malls, vans, and homes. It is also capable of providing standard treatment for all and there is no psychological burnout after the sixth client or student of the day. It continues to present its interactive dialogue in a totally objective way (if the author writes the program that way) without bias or stereotype related to the receiver or giver of the information and with the highest level of accuracy the system developer could achieve. This means that occupational descriptions, college descriptions, interpretation of tests and inventories, and assessments of probabilities of success, which are developed with the maximum of care and expertise, can be transmitted with high-quality, standardized treatment.

The ability of the computer to handle associated devices, such as the printer and the videodisc player, is also a powerful one. With the recent development of videodisc and other technology, the computer can supplement or replace its usual mode of "writing on the screen" with voice, color graphics, videotapes, motion pictures, and still pictures. This allows the delivery of a message in more than one medium making the learning more powerful. It also allows flexibility for various learning styles.

Cost effectiveness is another reason for utilizing computer technology. Unlike almost everything else today, the cost of computer hardware and software continues to decline as its capability continues to increase. Even if a top-of-the-line $6,000 microcomputer were purchased for use with students and only 1,200 uses were made in 1 year (200 school days times six uses per day), the per-hour use would only be $5. At this rate, the machine would be paid off in 1 year, and uses during the subsequent years would be no more expensive than $1 per hour, since this amount would pay for maintenance of hardware and even the most expensive software. With a national mean salary of $18,000 for counselors and $16,000 for teachers, the per-hour cost of counseling on a one-to-one basis is $9 and special education is $8 per hour per student. Clearly, computers and humans do not perform the same function, and the former should not replace the latter. However, there is an overlap in human and computer functions that the latter can perform as well as or better than humans at lower per-hour costs. Such overlapping functions should be delegated to computers.

Finally, but not least important, the studies of the results of computer-based career information and guidance systems indicate that they produce some very positive effects. These effects include increased knowledge about occupations and educational institutions, increased specificity of career plans, and increased vocational maturity and decision-making skills (as measured by paper and pencil instruments). A study (Garis, 1982) conducted at Pennsylvania State University compared three experimental groups and one control group on these variables. The control group was not allowed to receive any career guidance assistance from either computer or counselors for the period of the study. The three experimental groups had career guidance assistance in different modes: one group by computer alone, one group by counselor alone, and one group by a planned combination of the two. The scores on the outcome measures showed a consistent and statistically significant trend. The groups that received assistance by means of a combined program of computer and human services showed the greatest gains; the group that received assistance from computer alone made the next highest gains; and the group that received assistance from counselors alone was third in order and significantly lower than the other two. The control group had outcome measure scores much lower than the three experimental groups. This study was one of the first to examine effects of combined (i.e., human and computer treatment) treatment and is therefore significant.

Given a strong rationale for the use of the computer with all populations to enhance career development using motivational appeal, computer capabilities, cost effectiveness, and outcome effectiveness, attention is now turned to the purpose and content of career guidance and information systems.

PURPOSE AND CONTENT OF COMPUTER-BASED GUIDANCE AND INFORMATION SYSTEMS

The primary purpose of a computer-based career guidance or information system is to assist and support an individual in decision making. There are other modes of delivery of such support, namely one-to-one counseling, group guidance, curriculum, telephone, and printed self-help materials. As indicated by the research study cited above, the best treatment of an individual who is making career decisions is some optimum combination of these delivery modes. The discussion here, however, focuses on the computer as a delivery mode.

There are many planful or rational models of decision making. The one provided here (Figure 6.1) represents a synthesis of rational models presented in the psychology literature since the early 1950s. Several things should be noted about this "Planful Model." *First*, decision making is a process, not an event. This process can be defined in six discrete steps. *Second*, Steps 1–5 of the process are easily reversible whereas Step 6, the implementation of choice, is not reversible. The decider often moves from Step 2 to Step 3, for example, and then returns to Step 2, realizing that more self-information is needed before feasible alternatives can be generated. The collection of data about alternatives (Step 4) may have the effect of causing the decider to back up to Step 3 again in order to identify or create additional alternatives. *Third*, Steps 1–5 of the process are primarily internal to the individual and involve the use of mind, will, and emotion. Step 6 usually brings action that has impact external to the individual and causes concrete activity, bodily movement, and real expenditure of time, energy, and/or money. At this step commitment to a choice is at its highest point. *Fourth*, note that each of the six steps of the process requires, for optimal outcomes, the acquisition and processing of data. The following discussion expands on this theme and applies it to a computer-based career guidance or information system.

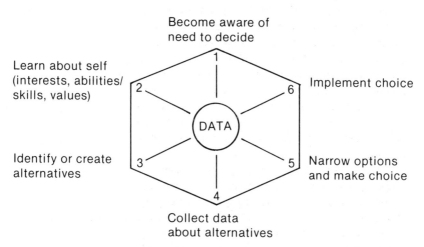

Figure 6.1.   Planful decision-making model: a synthesis.

Use of the Planful Model of Decision Making

The first step of the Planful Model—becoming aware of the need to decide—is perhaps the most difficult to effect in young people or adults who need to make career decisions; yet this step must occur first as the catalyst that empowers and triggers the decision-making process. The individual who is at psychological peace with the current state of affairs does not invest time and energy in the decision-making process. It is only when some dissatisfaction, imbalance, or need is experienced that the individual is willing to invest time, physical energy, and psychological energy in the deciding process. Often this step is triggered by the maturation process or an event that makes a connection for the individual between the now-present and the then-future, but it can also be triggered by data. Here, the definitional difference suggested by David Tiedeman (1972) is being used. That difference is that *data* are facts about options available to individuals, whereas *information* is the internalization of that data by a given individual for meaningful use in the decision-making process. Data such as the employment outlook in specific occupations, the percentage of college students who change majors, the percentage of college students who do not work in any field related to their under-graduate major, and the percentage of dissatisfied workers might trigger this awareness of need to decide. Computer files could conceivably contain such data, perhaps in a general instructional module on career development.

Donald Super (1963) proposed that the choice of an occupation is the implementation of a self-concept. Holland (1973), another eminent vocational choice theorist, stated that individuals develop interests in areas in which childhood and adolescent activities have been positively reinforced. Having an interest in a given area causes individuals to seek skills or competencies to perform well in these areas of interest. Finally, Holland presented the view that possessing a given set of interests and associated competencies has a causative effect on producing a set of compatible values. This combination of interests, competencies, and values gives persons a set of personality traits that can be implemented in occupations that utilize their interests and competencies and reward their values. This is another way of saying that an individual seeks to enter occupations that maximally "fit" the perception held of "self."

It therefore follows that a person will, or at least may, make an inappropriate vocational choice if the picture of self is not clear or accurate. Super (1963) described the dimensions and metadimensions of strong and "translatable" self-concepts. These dimensions include self-esteem (positive feelings toward self), clarity, refinement (degree of specificity of self-description), certainty, stability, and reality. The second step of the decision-making process—learning about self—is therefore a very critical one. Obviously, this self-learning comes from many sources, but a computer data file can be one of them. The types of self-information that may be attained in interactive dialogue with a computer data file are interests, abilities or skills, and important values, all based on interactions with on-line instruments or simulations. The identification, interpretation, and summary of these important self-variables can provide a firm base for the identification of potentially satisfying occupations. In this way, the computer utilizes its data files to provide information about the self for the user and to add clarity, refinement, stability, certainty, and reality to the self-concept.

In the third step of the planful process—identifying or creating alternatives—the computer again utilizes its data to assist the user. Computer-based career guidance and information systems offer searches of the occupational file by a variety of variables. One system provides a search only by values. Other systems offer searches by interests, abilities, job characteristics, majors and programs of study, and educational entry level. Assisting in this step of the deciding process is a very helpful and logical computer function. The computer has the unique ability to search large files by combinations of variables and to add or delete alternatives in an interactive way as the user becomes aware of the effects of each successive selected variable.

Support of the fourth step—collecting information about alternatives—is another very strong computer function. Because of the computer's abilities to store masses of data, to retrieve them quickly, to allow their update, and to display them either in printed form alone or in conjunction with audiovisual aids, the data collection phase of decision making is greatly enhanced. The use of computer files saves user time, has potential to offer more recently updated data, and provides a hard copy (by means of a printer attached to the cathode ray tube or TV screen) for the user to take away. Use of computer-based files offers the additional capability of allowing the user to ask for and retrieve a tailor-made subset of the total amount of information available about an occupation. In other words, the file can be made interactive, and the user can ask questions of it without the common problem of having to be exposed to more than is desired.

In the fifth step of the decision-making process—narrowing options— the computer is an excellent tool for pulling together the kind of data that will assist the user to apply a personal formula for narrowing available alternatives. This assistance with the narrowing process can come through the learning effect, which may be built into file search strategies and summaries. There are two common ways in which search strategies are performed on computer-based systems. In the first way, which requires less human and computer time, the user enters a number of variables desired in an occupation or a school all at one time. The computer then "overlays" a profile of the user's preferences (or it may be test scores) over the profiles of occupations or schools and identifies those which are a "match" or "near match." Depending upon the number of variables selected by the user and the size of the data file being accessed, the number of options identified may be few. Generation of the list of options informs the user about those that will satisfy the combination of all variables or preferences but will not teach the user the consequences of a string of choices or allow the user to reevaluate choices after learning about their consequences. For example, the user might enter the following variables in a search for 4-year colleges: location in the Middle Atlantic states, enrollment of no more than 5,000 students, state control, an SAT mean of 550, cost of not more than $5,000 per year, and a major in civil engineering. This particular search yields two colleges. The user would not realize from a search constructed in this way that the options were severely limited by the inconsistent combination of control, size, entrance score mean, and major. If, on the other hand, this same search were constructed so that the user enters one variable at a time and receives a report from the computer of the number of options in the file with that single variable only and in combination with all others previously entered, the user can be aware at the selection of each variable of the consequences of that choice. This seems to be a powerful guidance and learning function and a good example of turning data into information.

The second kind of function that can be built into computer software to assist individuals with the narrowing process is a summary function. The user may, for example, have searched an occupational data file by several variables, each independent of the other, such as interests, skills, values, and preferred job characteristics. After completion of four separate searches from different perspectives, it has a powerful capability to produce a combined list of the options for the user and to reveal the overlap. In other words, using the computer to assist the user to realize that, out of a list of 50 occupations that were generated from different searches, five relate to interests, skills, values, and job characteristics in combination is another powerful way of turning data into information. The user should thus be informed that these occupations have very high priority for detailed exploration since they have higher potential to be satisfying ones than others that may relate only to one or two of the self-variables entered.

Another way the computer can assist with the narrowing process is by the provision of some of the reality testing that individuals need to do before committing to an occupational or educational choice. There are shades of reality testing ranging from reading about a possible option, to observing it, to experiencing it through on-site visitation or direct involvement in activities. The computer can help with such reality testing through printed information, work experience simulation, and audiovisual presentation of the workplace and tasks.

Finally, we move to the computer's role in assisting people with the implementation of tentative choices. At this stage of the decision-making process, relatively more emphasis is given by the decider to action-oriented steps than to internal psychological processes. In relation to career decision making, these action steps usually involve the finding of a job or source of financial aid, or entrance into a school or military program. Because the plethora of options related to these alternatives is vast, the computer again serves a valuable search and retrieval function. Individuals may select from more than 3,500 2- and 4-year institutions, 11,000 approved proprietary schools, or 450 military training programs. The computer can assist the individual in making good choices regarding the implementation process because of its ability to: select only those options with characteristics desired by the decider; compare the same categories of information across options; provide detailed information about next steps for entry; and provide audiovisual support material to give close to real-life data about available options.

GUIDANCE VERSUS INFORMATION SYSTEMS IN RELATION TO THE DECISION-MAKING MODEL

There are currently several actively marketed computer-based systems designed to assist individuals with career development and/or vocational choice. Conceptually, these systems can be divided into two groups: those designed to be information systems and those designed to be guidance systems. There are at least three basic differences between these two types. First, information systems seek to utilize the computer to search large files with a combination of many variables and to provide detailed information about those options that are identified by the search. Guidance systems have these same functions but are not limited to these functions only. Second, information systems devote little or no time to the collection of information about the self, whereas guidance systems inevitably devote major attention to the user's interests, abilities, and/or values in order to relate these data to available options. Third, information systems do not propose any given method or formula for decision making; rather, they provide the grist for it. Guidance systems, on the other hand, propose either directly or indirectly a specified process for making vocational and educational decisions and utilize the computer as a monitor to help the decider use this process. Information systems, therefore, are sophisticated tools that feed data into the individual's deciding process upon request. Guidance systems, on the other hand, not only provide much of the needed data for decision making, but also propose, monitor, and support a specified decision-making process that includes the acquisition of relevant self-data.

APPLICABILITY OF COMPUTER CAPABILITIES TO SPECIAL POPULATIONS

There are other unique capabilities of the computer that can assist individuals in special target populations with career development and choice. First, consider the possible positive effects of the use of computer-based systems with women. There are several aspects of a computer-based system that must be "fair" in order to declare it free of sex bias. These include the data files, the instruments used in the system, and the audiovisual materials that may enhance it. Data files include both the interactive dialogue between the user and the computer and the descriptions of occupations and educational institutions. With careful writing, data files can be developed to provide absolutely standard information about an occupation and its requirements (to both men and women) without any of the subtle bias often transmitted by humans in verbal or nonverbal communication. If the system administers and interprets interest or ability measures, these too must meet the ethical guidelines for sex fairness in terms of face validity, item selection, norming, and interpretation. Finally, associated manuals, slides, videodiscs, or audio-visual materials must also reflect the same quality of sex fairness by showing both sexes performing a variety of work tasks and by failing to reinforce the established stereotypes about occupations "appropriate" for members of either sex. One outstanding capability of the computer is to present a predetermined treatment to all individuals irrespective of race, sex, or handicap, with consistency and without any of the alterations that humans provide.

Computer-based systems are an ideal mode of delivery for the deaf and hard-of-hearing. For most applications, the delivery of text on a printer, cathode ray tube, or TV screen is sufficient. Given the language handicap characteristic of many deaf and hard-of-hearing individuals, text and files used with other populations may have to be written at a lower reading level. For some applications, the addition of signing may be desirable. This can be done by utilizing a videodisc under computer control that overlays the signing on the pictorial and textual material.

Low-cost "black boxes" are now available that can translate computer text to artificial voice. This technology makes it possible for blind persons to interact with the computer by hearing the interactive text and responding via braille-marked keys. Braille printers offer a second alternative for computer-person interaction because they print computer text and files in braille.

The computer can also provide unique assistance to individuals at both ends of the learning ability continuum. Computer interaction and text can be written and stored in two or more reading and comprehension levels. Based upon user entry of data or checking of data within a user record, the system can provide the interaction at an appropriate reading level. Because videodiscs can store two tracks of sound, it is also possible for a computer-accessed videodisc to "talk" in either of two different languages or comprehension levels.

There is another type of differentiation that the computer can address. This is the vast differentiation in vocational maturity that deciders may bring to the computer terminal. It is well known that individuals vary widely in their ability to cope with career-related developmental tasks. Super (1974) stated that vocational maturity is a blend of the factors of awareness of need to plan, decision-making skill, knowledge and use of informational resources, possession of general career and world-of-work information, and possession of specific occupational information. Super and others have developed instruments to measure vocational maturity. Such instruments could be administered on-line at the first sign-on for a given user. The user could then be directed to specific parts within the system based upon specific needs identified and/or level of vocational maturity possessed.

In developing a career guidance system to meet the needs of special populations, the question always arises as to whether or not the computer should be used as a screening tool to help determine which occupations are appropriate for people with given handicaps. Because it is entirely feasible to code occupations by characteristics such as the optimal eyesight needed, the level of hearing required, and optimal intelligence level, it is possible to compare objective data about the user with characteristic requirements of the occupations. Such a search strategy would mask out occupational titles considered inappropriate for individuals with specific handicapping conditions. Although technically feasible, I have conceptually denied this approach. My preference is for a system that assists all individuals to identify occupations that relate to personal interests, abilities, and values, irrespective of handicapping conditions. Once these occupational titles are identified, the physical and mental requirements should be accurately represented in the detailed occupational information. From these data, the handicapped individual should evaluate his or her ability to cope with the work tasks, and the potential employer should consider the degree to which the usual work environment and tasks can be modified to accommodate the handicapped individual. This approach seems more equitable than allowing the computer to eliminate occupations from consideration, since both the individual and the environment might be capable of accommodation.

POSITIVE EFFECTS TO BE EXPECTED

The research on computer-based career guidance and information systems has consistently shown that use of the computer alone for career assistance will produce significant positive effects. Use of the computer in conjunction with human services, however, produces more important and significant effects (Garis, 1982) than use of the computer alone or human treatment alone. All studies of computer-based career guidance and information systems validate a very high level of acceptance of such systems by users (Arnold, 1978;) (Chapman, Katz, Norris, & Pear, 1977;) (Myers et al., 1972), and a preference for receiving information by computer over receipt of information from printed or microfiche materials (Fredericksen, 1978; Ross, 1971; Weick, 1972). Use of computer-based systems for 4 hours or more produces the following effects:

1. Users can state a higher level of specificity of career plans.
2. Users have more cognitive knowledge about the occupations or schools that they research on the system.
3. Users report a higher level of self-understanding.
4. Users engage in a larger number and range of exploratory activities than nonusers. Such exploratory activities include writing for more information, using other kinds of files in the career library, talking to parents and other significant adults about career planning, and talking to counselors.
5. Users request more service from counselors than nonusers, but the level of information and assistance sought is at a significantly higher level.
6. Users make some gains in vocational maturity and decision-making skills, as measured by appropriate instruments.
7. Users will return an average of three to four times when left to do so voluntarily.

SOME PROBLEMS TO BE EXPECTED

A very bright picture has been painted for the use of the computer in career guidance and information, but no mode of delivery of information or services is devoid of its characteristic problems and frustrations. One of the primary liabilities of computer-based systems is the tendency for counselors to ignore them. By nature and choice, most counselors prefer to work with people on a one-to-one basis in a mode that capitalizes on warmth, trust, and empathy. Characteristically, counselors are attuned to the solution of problems through use of verbal skills and the power of good communication. Technology is both feared and mistrusted by many counselors, and counselor education programs have not been designed or modified to ameliorate the lack of knowledge and the negative attitudes about use of computer technology. The result is that a computer-based system is often installed without the permission or involvement of guidance personnel. For that reason, it is not welcomed or incorporated as a valuable tool to be used with many others to help in the delivery of a systematic program. It is viewed as intrusive, if not unwanted. That perception alone greatly reduces its potential effectiveness. Students will receive the benefits already enumerated if it is used, but there will not be the added support by humans, which is critical to maximal effectiveness. In-service training and the deliberate construction of programs to include the computer as one mode of delivery in a total systematic program of services are essential.

The second area of expected problems relates to technical concerns. Some problems with priority, phone lines, down time, and program bugs are inevitable in a system of timesharing on a mini- or maxicomputer. The best solution for all of these problems is to establish a good relationship with data processing personnel assigned to support the guidance operation. The microcomputer offers the potential for less frustration since problems of priority, phone lines, and down time are largely eliminated.

SUMMARY

This chapter has reviewed both the rationale for the use of the computer in guidance and the components of a systematic career guidance program. These have subsequently been cast into a planful decision-making model. The potential of the computer to assist individuals to internalize this model has been reviewed, and distinctions have been drawn between information systems and guidance systems. Some attention has been given to the applicability of computer support to the special populations with whom this text is concerned. Finally, some expected positive effects and problems have been cited that will be further amplified in other chapters in this text.

REFERENCES

Arnold, W. (1978). *Evaluation of the Georgia Career Information System as used at pilot demonstration sites*. Available from author through Georgia State University.

Chapman, W., Katz, M. R., Norris, L., & Pears, L. (1977). *Field test and evaluation of a computer-based system of interactive guidance and information*. Princeton, NJ: Educational Testing Service.

Fredericksen, G. (1978). SIGI utilization through June 23, 1978 (Memorandum). Available from author at California State Polytechnic University, Pomona, California.

Garis, J. W. (1982). *The integration of a computer-based guidance system in a college counseling center: Its effects upon career planning*. Unpublished doctoral dissertation, Pennsylvania State University, University Park.

Holland, J. L. (1973). *Making vocational choices*. Englewood Cliffs, NJ: Prentice-Hall.

Myers, R. A. et al. (1972). *Educational and career exploration system: Report of a two-year field trial*. New York: Teachers' College Press.

Ross, L. L. (1971). *The effectiveness of two systems for delivering occupational information: A comparative analysis*. Master's thesis, University of Oregon, Eugene.

Super, D. E. (1963). *Career development: Self-concept theory*. New York: College Entrance Examination Board.

Super, D. E. (1974). Vocational Maturity Theory: Toward Implementing A Psychology of Careers and Career Education and Guidance. In *Measuring vocational maturity for counseling and evaluation*. Washington, DC: National Vocational Guidance Association.

Tiedeman, D. V. (1972). Can a machine develop a career? A structure for the epigenesis of self-realization in career development. In J. M. Whiteley and A. Resnikoff (eds.), *Perspectives on vocational development*. Washington, DC: American Personnel and Guidance Association.

Weick, J. (1972). *Occupational information for employment service counseling: An evaluation of Occupational Information Access System pilot use in three Portland Employment Division offices*. Eugene: University of Oregon.

7

The Computer as a Tool for Providing Career Development to the Handicapped

Charles W. Humes and Lee Joyce Richmond

There are multiple ways in which the computer can be used as a tool for providing career development skills for the handicapped. The age of high technology is causing a radical shift in the way society views humankind. In the industrial era, value was placed on humans as workers. In the communications era, the value of a person is more likely to be measured by how that person relates with others. Career is no longer narrowly conceived as a job, but rather—more broadly conceived as life (Tiedeman, Miller-Tiedeman & Carhart, 1983). Here, the handicapped and non-handicapped alike would share in the career development process, continually differentiating (separating out) and reintegrating (bringing together again) their individual identities as they form and reform them through experience (Tiedeman & O'Hara, 1963).

High technology advances those experiences. Through the computer, with its information services and simulated resources, the handicapped individual can explore and interact with the world. This capability, coupled with the concept of career as a total life construct, will surely influence the self-actualization capacities of the disabled. But this is the future. How does the computer apply today to the career development of the handicapped youth in our schools and colleges?

As educators speculate on the effects of the new technology, it is apparent that it affects education in two basic ways: (1) intelligent machines demand different cognitive skills; and (2) the learning process is changing. These general trends impact special education and handicapped students in the same proportions as they affect regular education. Before addressing the influence on the handicapped, however, it is useful to review the impact on general education.

The new technology influences how we learn, what we learn, and where we learn. In order to understand the pervasiveness of this influence, it is necessary to understand something about the new technology. The new technology deals with microelectronics, communications, and information science. Microelectronics perform traditional tasks, such as filtering signals, but they can also carry out logical operations. Electronic communication involves digital coding of voice, video, data messages, and microelectronic switching. Information science, the software, creates the material for the hardware implied.

Applications of the new technology, if now visionary in large part, are fast becoming a reality as a result of reduced costs and convergence (Johnson, 1981). Computer costs are decreasing by 30% per year, and communication costs are falling at 20%. At the same time, the new technology is converging with other technologies (e.g., television, motion pictures, and data processing). These trends are rapidly putting the new technology within the reach of every educational institution, no matter how small or isolated.

APPLICATION TO THE HANDICAPPED

There are two assumptions that one must make in approaching the notion of using the new technology with the handicapped. First, whatever is applicable and relevant for general education is equally so for special education; second, services to the handicapped are here to stay regardless of political and legislative vagaries. The problem is to know how to wed the two in order to promote efficiency and effectiveness. The use of the microcomputer for regular populations is now extensively documented. There are more than 100,000 computers in the nation's schools (Friederich, 1983). Specialized use, such as in the career development of the nonhandicapped, has slowly started to emerge (Chapman & Katz, 1983). Although some of the same strategies can be used—for example, motivational appeal and instant access to vast arrays of information, or the use of computerized information and guidance systems—when applied to career counseling of the handicapped, they can be taken a step further. It is necessary to relate the new technology to some of the specific and unique considerations of this population. Although such strategies may apply to handicapped persons of all ages, they are most applicable to the school-age population. This is true, in part, because of the current availability of computerized systems for this population, the dynamic developmental stages of young people, and the intervention potential of these systems.

In any discussion of the handicapped, it is critical to point out that this total population is exceedingly heterogeneous and must be considered in terms of subpopulations. According to the 1977 P.L. 94-142 regulations, the population includes the mentally retarded, hard-of-hearing, deaf, speech-impaired, visually handicapped, seriously emotionally disturbed, orthopedially impaired, other health impaired, deaf-blind, multihandicapped, and other learning disabled. Thus, there are vast differences, both intergroup and intragroup, within the total population.

THE COMPUTER AS A TOOL

Although it is useful to examine general issues and specific concerns regarding enhancing career development for the handicapped, it is more pragmatic to look at computerized systems as tools for solving some of the generic problems that affect the handicapped in the area of career development. These problems are ubiquitous and are bothersome to special educators and counselors who have been charged with the responsibility of facilitating career development skills.

It is certainly fair to say that career development of the handicapped has lagged because of career stereotypes of the handicapped (Humes, 1982). Among the stereotypes are those that propose that career development with the handicapped is unsystematic, unimportant, inherently limited, arrested, and stressful. Elements of these stereotypes are based in folklore, but other aspects are related to difficulties encountered in attempting to deal with generic problems. Some of these generic problem areas are listed here and are followed by a discussion of computer applications.

Assessment

Although testing has always played a prominent part in the lives of handicapped persons, presumably to assess strengths rather than weaknesses, it took P.L. 94-142 to ensure that assessment would be an integral component of the educational experiences of handicapped students. One of the mandates of this national statute requires an assessment of the student's current functioning. Certain provisions of the regulations are revealing:

> Tests are selected and administered so as to best insure that when a test is

administered to a child with impaired sensory, manual, or speaking skills, the test results accurately reflect the child's aptitude or achievement level or whatever other functions the test purports to measure, rather than reflecting the child's impaired sensory, manual, or speaking skills (except where those skills are the factors which the test purports to measure) (Federal Register, 1977, pp. 42495–42497)

The implications in this statement are very clear. Primary considerations must be given each child and every effort should be made to assess by such instruments or decisions as will legitimately determine the current level of functioning. Tests, in general, come under heavy fire as biased and discriminatory. Such overall concerns are particularly applicable to the handicapped. Interestingly, but not surprisingly, most test adaptations have been designed for the visually and hearing impaired (Lombana, 1981), where it has been possible to adapt pencil-and-paper tests to these impairments. Beyond this, nothing much has happened. However, with the advent of the computer and the possibilities engendered by the keyboard and stylus, other variations are now possible.

Information Management

As counselors or special educators approach career development strategies for handicapped students, they find themselves burdened and frustrated by mountains of paperwork. This paperwork was occasioned by the regulations associated with P.L. 94-142, but the blame cannot be placed there alone. Any effort to individualize instruction or educational strategies must inevitably lead to the monitoring of individual progress. (This notable objective is one of the Catch-22 elements of the legislation.) The individualized education program (IEP) is perhaps the first major breakthrough in the individualization of instruction for the handicapped. So much so, in fact, that parents of "nonhandicapped" students who have no such provision view it with envy. Because the IEP does require the written specification of goals, objectives, and evaluative criteria, it leads to the proliferation of paperwork. The only reasonable way to manage the data base maintenance implied is through a system of computer-managed instruction (CMI). One example of a CMI global approach is MICRO-CMI (McIsaac & Baker, 1981). The available options in the package include performance profile reports, student grouping functions, student grading, data base maintenance, listings and reports, programs of studies, curriculum maintenance, diagnosis/prescription, and test scoring. With such a vast array of information available it is now possible to manage that information and to translate it into meaningful career development strategies via the IEP. The motivation behind the general concept of CMI was accountability. This certainly lends itself to the management of programs for handicapped students when administrators, teachers, and counselors are required to defend judgments and decisions on individual student learning programs. The time will come when every special educator and counselor will have on his or her desk a microcomputer that will immediately furnish past information and be ready to process new information.

Evaluations

Akin to information management is evaluation. In this era of account-ability, policy makers and budget developers are insisting on more emphasis on measuring the quality of services. Their clarion cry usually relates to outcome-oriented measures. In terms of career development strategies for the handicapped, the evaluation can encompass IEP objectives, student self-assessment, or problem-solving skills. Evaluation applied to IEP objectives and student self-assessment speaks for itself, but the process applied to problem-solving activity may not. Microcomputers are ideally suited to the latter type of evaluation activity. Computers are analytical problem-solving tools (Eisele, 1981). Because of this, the simple modeling of the analytical process will often generalize to other problem-solving skills. The career development paradigm is essentially a problem-solving exercise, and material can be presented that deals with problem identification, hypothesis formulation, solution testing, and solution selection. The process supports a variety of learning styles, and progress can be evaluated at any point in the paradigm. Self-evaluation conducted in this interactive way is not only painless but motivational. The handicapped person, often frustrated and bitter, needs motivational appeal and a friendly support system like the microcomputer.

Information and Guidance Systems

Computer information system is a term that describes a standardized procedure for computer-based obtaining, filing, and disseminating of information. Systems of varying complexities have been developed to provide career information for the handicapped. As pointed out in Chapter 6 by Harris-Bowlsbey, these can be categorized as either information or guidance systems. Regrettably, it is often assumed that such systems are not appropriate for the handicapped. Computers can perform several, but not all, career-guidance tasks, and the same constraints would apply for use with the handicapped. The two tasks that are amenable to computer systems are exploration of educational and career options and imple-mentation of choice. Some of the better known computer systems that have applicability to the handicapped are discussed here.

System of Interactive Guidance and Information (SIGI)   This is a
system designed for junior college students. It contains six subsystems (values, locate, compare, prediction, planning, and strategy).
Two-hundred and twenty occupations can be analyzed in terms of the
subsystems. Vocabulary is geared to the 8th grade level so its use
with the handicapped would be restricted to those with satisfactory
academic functioning.

Career Information System (CIS)   This system allows a person to
explore occupations related to self-assessed interests and abilities.
The system, originally based in Oregon, taps a data file of 240
occupations. It allows recovery of 300-word summaries of duties,
outlook, and working conditions. The system has proven useful in
public school, higher education, and community settings. Handicapped persons using the system should have functional reading
capacity.

Guidance Information System (GIS)   Formerly called the Interactive
Learning System, this system contains four information banks that
the users can question to receive information. The files are: (1)
occupational; (2) 4-year college; (3) 2-year college; and (4) scholar-
ship and financial aid. The system has audiovisual filmstrips and
cassettes that offer motivational appeal for handicapped persons
(e.g., the learning disabled).

Experimental Education and Career Exploration System (ECES)
This approach is heralded as the first complete computer-based
career development system. It is based on Super's paradigm of
vocational development. The system provides five steps through
which students progress: (1) awareness; (2) search; (3) explore; (4)
experience; and (5) plan. It seems to have equal applicability to both
the college and noncollege bound. The system has been well received
by disadvantaged populations, and it should have usefulness for a
broad spectrum of the handicapped.

Computerized Vocational Information System (CVIS)   This broad-
based system can be used at both the junior and senior high school
levels. The student can explore colleges, specialized schools,
apprenticeships, jobs, and military options. It has data on about 400
occupations and uses Roe's fields-by-levels occupational classification. It has been used successfully with economically disadvantaged vocational students and should have applicability to lower
functioning handicapped students.

Discover   This third-generation system, in addition to information and
interaction, has the capability to simulate exercises in values
clarification and decision making, and to perform on-line administration and interpretation of tests. Evaluation data suggest that the

system can help students specify career plans, understand occupations, and increase self-understanding. It can be used with both junior and senior high students. It has high motivational appeal and has the capacity to provide a personal experience. Such a system has much potential with a wide range of handicapped students.

It is apparent that most of the above information systems, in present format, are most applicable to those handicapped persons with an adequate academic education who aspire to post-high school training. These parameters would certainly apply to many (perhaps a great many) handicapped youths. However, with modifications, these or similar systems could have relevance for even a broader base of the handicapped population. If reading is a problem, graphics might be appropriately used. The microcomputer permits local adaptations of commercial systems that can meet the needs of discrete populations. However, a good information system for the handicapped will only be as effective in career development for the handicapped as a good counselor permits it to be.

Computer-assisted Instruction

Although computer-assisted instruction (CAI) may on the surface seem unrelated to career development for the handicapped, a close examination reveals that it is essential in terms of improving basic skill development. Without the basic skills, especially reading, the more limited of the handicapped will have a difficult time utilizing the several commercial systems. CAI was popular in the 1960s and lost its high appeal in the 1970s (Holmes, 1982). The advent of the microcomputer has reawakened interest in this most basic of all computer applications. In addition to providing remediation, drill and practice, and information for the handicapped, CAI can make positive improvements in educational environments and a contribution to the establishment of "least restriction" in those settings.

One of the persistent barriers to effective use of CAI is teacher attitudes. The counselor can play a key role in teacher acceptance of CAI strategies for the handicapped by emphasizing that this educational strategy can increase student motivation and competence and, furthermore, that the new technology will not dehumanize the teaching process. Obviously, in order to carry out this consultative function counselors must believe these statements to be true.

In the same vein, counselors must not assume that handicapped students will automatically embrace computer technology. Although nonhandicapped students tend to be receptive to change, the same cannot be said for their handicapped counterparts. The handicapped, as a group, have probably more fears, suspicions, and ingrained habits. These may be caused by the handicap itself, but it is more likely that they are sequelae to failure or overprotection. The counselor must ensure that the handicapped learner has proper orientation to the hardware, easy access to machines, and immediate feedback. Although self-instruction is valuable, the handicapped student will probably be more receptive if CAI supplements traditional modes of instruction. It should be remembered that some of the handicapped subpopulations (e.g., learning disabled and emotionally disturbed) have inherent self-motivational problems and sequencing difficulties.

GLIMPSES OF THE FUTURE

For the handicapped worker, the future may well be the best of times. We will live in a world where, for example, a TRS-80 computer can, at very low cost, replace a teletypewriter and be used as a portable tele-communication system for the deaf by storing, transmitting, and receiving messages over any telephone. We will live in a world where lipreading can be taught by means of converting typed sentences into animated mouth movements, thereby serving as a training aid to the teaching of lipreading. Moreover, we will live in a world where any controlled movement that can activate a switch can enable users of a computer communication assister to have their thoughts printed on a screen or paper, and spoken by the computer itself through a voice synthesizer. These devices are not hypothetical constructs, but presently existing tools. They are examples of the winning entries in the Johns Hopkins First National Search on Personal Computing to Aid the Handicapped.[1]

There is no question that the computer is a tool that can aid the career development of the handicapped. It can help one think, clean one's house, cook one's food, speak one's thoughts, and be one's arms and eyes. It can, in fact, bring the world of the nonhandicapped to the handicapped and enable them to function in it despite their disability.

An example of what is possible is part of the General Motors exhibit at the EPCOT Center in Florida. The exhibit houses an automobile that has no steering wheel, no gas pedal, and no side-view mirrors. The front window is merely decorative. Inside the car is a screen that monitors the road. The car is controlled by push buttons and its systems are monitored at all times by a computer. A right hemisphere stroke victim who cannot

---

[1] For a brief description of the three entries described see Levitt, Hight, and Crookston, respectively, in *The Johns Hopkins APL Technical Digest*, July-September, 1982, *3*(3), 273.

walk and has moderate visual impairment could safely and comfortably drive such a vehicle.

For the handicapped student/worker of the future, computers can be used in the following five ways: as an information source, an instructional delivery tool, a management tool, a communication device, and a physical aid. In each instance, technology can help the handicapped person compensate for developmental lags caused by the handicapping condition.

In its traditional use as an informational source, the computer can store large data bases that can be easily accessed. The previously mentioned career information systems (CVIS, SIGI, COIN, GIS, Discover, and others) can be updated to contain information about occupations particularly suitable for the handicapped. These systems can also provide information about institutions of higher learning that make provision for the particular training needs of persons with specific disabilities. A little known fact is that some colleges make special arrangements for learning-disabled students; others have programs for the deaf, and still others for the physically impaired. What is needed—and is something the future will bring—is a computerized educational and occupational information system for the handicapped frequently updated with local and national data bases.

As an instructional delivery tool, the computer will serve as an advanced media device. Imagine a student sitting at a desk-top personal computer that is connected to a videotape or videodisc machine. The program is a business program focused on banking; the student is learning international finance. Instead of working with a keyboard, the student, who has arm and fingers paralysis, uses a light pen which she holds in her mouth to indicate a response. She receives immediate feedback.

The branching capabilities of the program enable her to ask for further information or clarification, or to call for more difficult examples and questions. The instruction is entirely individualized, and the student moves at her own pace to acquire knowledge and skills in an occupation in which she anticipates a bright future. The instructional program alone is a thing of the future. The interactive video instruction system is a currently available training tool.

Computers and other electromechanical technologies have the potential to be the springboard to successful living for the handicapped. Free of social bias, the computer does not discriminate among its users, nor does it give negative feedback unless programmed to do so. When the computer indicates that an error has been made, it does not hurt the user's ego or self-concept. It is therefore a safe teaching device for youths and adults who want to try to venture where they have never been before.

At best, however, the future does not presage an industrial society with emphasis on material growth and on learning for the "real world of work" in which persons serve institutions. Rather, it more probably offers a transindustrial paradigm where there is emphasis on human growth and development, and where concern with the frontiers of the human mind and spirit will become more manifest. In such a model, institutions serve people and learning is lifelong. In the society of the future, the computer, in conjunction with additional electromechanical devices, can help individuals overcome their physical limitations.

If there is a future for any of us in a thermonuclear age, there will be a future for all of us. Technology has the potential to prove the handicapped no exception to this forecast.

REFERENCES

Chapman, W., & Katz, M. R. (1983). Career information systems in secondary schools: A survey and assessment. *Vocational Guidance Quarterly*, *31*, 165–177.

Eisele, J. E. (1981). Computers in the schools: Now that we have them . . . ? *Educational Technology*, *21*, 24–27.

Federal Register. (1977, August 23), 42496–42497. Washington, D.C.: U.S. Government Printing Office.

Friederich, O. (1983, Janaury 3). The computer moves in. *Time*, pp. 76–82.

Holmes, G. (1982). Computer-assisted instruction: A discussion of some of the issues for would-be implementors. *Educational Technology*, *22*,7–13.

Humes, C. W. (1982). Career guidance for the handicapped—A comprehensive approach. *Vocational Guidance Quarterly*, *30*, 351–358.

Johnson, J. W. (1981). Education and the new technology: A force of history. *Educational Technology*, *21*, 15–23.

Lombana, J. (1981). *Guidance for handicapped students*. Springfield, IL: Charles C Thomas.

McIsaac, D. N., & Baker, F. B. (1981). Computer-managed instruction system implementation on a microcomputer. *Educational Technology*, *21*, 40–46.

Tiedeman, D. V., & O'Hara, R. P. (1963). *Career development: Choice and adjustment*, Princeton, NJ: College Entrance Examination Board.

Tiedeman, D. V., Miller-Tiedeman, A., & Carhart, R. (1983). Oops, the world just experienced our mindquakes in career. *Cognica*, *14*(7): 1–3.

8

Counselor Education Programs
Training for Career Development with Exceptional People

Edwin L. Herr

The conventional literature on counselor education is relatively silent about training for career development for exceptional people. Reviews of such journals of *Counselor Education and Supervision*, the *Personnel and Guidance Journal*, and the *Vocational Guidance Quarterly* yield virtually no articles during the past 15 years focused specifically on this important issue.

It could be assumed that one would find extensive coverage in the rehabilitation literature on counselor training for career development for exceptional people. But, here, too, one finds relative silence. Rehabilitation journals, like some of the journals cited above, periodically produce articles that speak to the practices important to facilitating career development in selected populations of exceptional people; these articles typically do not address dimensions of the training of counselors necessary to such practices, however.

One can conclude from a review of the literature that if the frequency and focus of published articles are an indication of the content of counselor education, little attention is given to models of training or to related research questions that address the training of counselors for career development for exceptional people. Conversely, the actual practice and research concerned with the career development of exceptional persons seems to be more advanced.

SOME PRESENT PERSPECTIVES ON
COUNSELOR EDUCATION

Given the above perspective on the current and rather limited state of the literature in general, it is useful, nevertheless, to examine the substance of a few of the available views on counselor education's role in training counselors for career development for exceptional people. In 1979, the *Personnel and Guidance Journal* published a special issue on counseling handicapped persons and their families. Two articles addressed career education and career counseling with handicapped persons (Brolin & Gysbers, 1979; Sinick, 1979).

In addition, that special issue included one article devoted to preparing counselors to meet the needs of the handicapped (Hosie, 1979). Although the article did not focus primarily on the issue of training in career development for exceptional persons, such an emphasis was discussed. Keying primarily upon the effects on counselors of P.L. 94-142, The Education for All Handicapped Children Act, Hosie contended that counselors must become competent in a number of areas through pre- or in-service training. In order to provide comprehensive service to handicapped populations he believed that counselors at least need such knowledge and skills as the following:

1. Federal and state legislation, guidelines, and local policies relating to programs and services for the handicapped.
2. Rights of handicapped children and their parents, and the skills necessary to advise parents and enable them to exercise their rights.
3. State guidelines for classification, diagnostic tools and their limitations, and the skills necessary to relate these to learning characteristics and the common elements of correction.
4. Informal assessment procedures, and the skills necessary to relate these to the special learning strategies of the handicapped.
5. Growth and development process, characteristics, and impediments of the handicapped, and the skills necessary to relate this knowledge to developmental learning tasks and strategies.
6. Characteristics and development of the learning disabled, and the skills necessary to diagnose why the individual is failing tasks and to change methods and objectives when necessary.
7. Sensory impairments, speech disorders, and communication deficits, their effect on diagnosis and remediation, and the skills

necessary to overcome or lessen their effect in learning and counseling settings.

8. Input, structure, and potential outcomes of the Individual Education Program (I.E.P.), and the skills necessary to consult and assist in their construction for the mainstreamed student.

9. Ability, learning rates, and modes of learning of the handicapped, and the skills necessary to utilize these factors in recommending educational placements and environments.

10. Attitudinal biases of teachers and others, and the skills necessary to teach and consult with regular and special educators to produce a facilitative learning environment.

11. Learning disorders, the social and emotional behavior problems of handicapped students, and the skills necessary to instruct and consult with teachers, using behavior modification and management principles to enhance academic learning and social behavior.

12. Potential growth and development of the handicapped child; fears, concerns, and needs of the parents; and the skills necessary to consult, counsel, and teach children regarding methods to facilitate their child's academic and social development.

13. Characteristics of the handicapped related to employment skills, training programs, and potential occupational and educational opportunities, and the skills necessary to assist the individual in career decision making and development.

14. Roles and skills of other personnel within and outside the institution, and the skills necessary to refer them or work with them to enhance the learning and development of the handicapped individual. (pp. 271–272).

Although Hosie, quoting some of his own research (Vandergriff & Hosie, 1979), goes on to argue that counselor approaches to working with handicapped students are more similar to than different from approaches with nonhandicapped students (p. 272), presumably this view assumes that counselors first have acquired the specific types of understanding arrayed in the 14 areas previously quoted (i.e., their approaches are implemented within such a base of knowledge and sensitivity to the particular needs of the handicapped).

In characterizing the major types of content that counselors need, Hosie particularly emphasized parental counseling, assessment and learning, rules and regulations, behavior modification, and career counseling and needs. Regarding the latter, he wrote primarily about reference materials concerned with vocational preparation, services, placement, and evaluation of handicapped persons, with which counselors should be familiar. He further cited the need for counselors to be prepared to modify the learning environment in existing academic and vocational programs. He also recommended specific counselor education instructional designs through which counselor competence in career development for handicapped person can be achieved.

Hosie's suggestions about what should be included in counselor preparation programs tend to agree with Lombana's (1980) findings in which 195 school counselors in Florida described areas of needed in-service programs with respect to their activities with handicapped students.

Humes (1978) also has addressed the effects of P.L. 94-142 on counselors, especially school counselors. He contended that "many counselors are not prepared, philosophically or by background for the roles [required of them by P.L. 94-142]. . . . Certainly, counselor training in the past 10 years has not dealt with this new set of expectations" (p. 126).
He indicated that the:

> burden for the provision of both in-service and preservice activities for school counselors will rest with counselor education . . . One issue will be to what extent the traditional model of counselor training should be changed to reflect the emerging needs generated by P.L. 94-142. We may assume that most counselor educators will continue to endorse the precept of serving the developmental needs of all students. Undoubtedly, some techniques and strategies related to implementation of the law may be incorporated into existing course offerings. (p. 127).

Humes went on to argue that particular topics that need to be incorporated in counselor education are IEPs, a least-restrictive environment, due process procedures, confidentiality of information, and vocational counseling. With respect to the latter, he indicated that "vocational counseling for the handicapped will be different from that for the nonhandicapped and will require different options and alternatives." Such observations point out the need for counselor education to respond to such matters, but give little guidance in how to do so.

COUNSELOR ATTITUDES TOWARD THE DISABLED

The issue of attitude is an important matter in counselor preparation. Evidence exists that the general lay population, a variety of undergraduate and graduate students, and rehabilitation personnel do, in fact, have preferences, prejudices, and value systems relevant to their relationships with such groups as former mental patients, blacks, and the disabled (Bell, 1962; Lamy, 1966; Tringo, 1968; Vontress, 1970). There are observers who would argue that it is not the techniques or approaches to stereotyping that need to be different in counseling with handicapped rather than nonhandicapped populations. Instead, the issue is the counselor's attitude toward exceptionalities, cultural, racial, or sexual differences. For example, Fix and Rohrbacker (1977) noted that "disabled people often discuss the fact that the disability is not so much a functional limitation as it is the negative attitude of others" (p. 176). They then reported a series of workshops designed to eliminate barriers between counselors and handicapped persons. A major part of the process of attitude change is having the workshop participants engage in activities— shopping, using vending machines, using bathroom facilities, crossing streets, using public water fountains, summarizing or engaging in conversations—while portraying the functional limitations occasioned by deafness, paraplegia, visual impairment, or other disabilities. The evaluations of the workshops suggested new insights, and changed participants' perceptions of people who are physically disabled.

Ibrahim and Herr (1982) examined the different effects of experiential and informational approaches in modifying attitudes of potential "helpers" toward disabled persons and the continuing effect of attitude modification toward disabled persons over a 6-week period of time. The participants in the experiential mode were asked to role play in pairs a specific disability from the area of speech pathology or audiology (e.g., stuttering, articulation problems, or some other speech or hearing handicap) for a period of 5 hours. The participants in the informational group were exposed to films, slide shows, written personal accounts of disabled individuals, and discussions of problems and prejudices encountered by the handicapped. Results indicated significantly positive attitudes toward the disabled in the treatment groups, with the experiential treatment having the greatest impact.

There are other types of workshops described in the professional literature in either preservice or in-service formats that focus upon the attitudes of professionals about various types of exceptionalities, cross-cultural perspectives, or stereotyping (see, e.g., Pederson, Holwill, & Shapiro, 1978). There is at least one article (Ioracchini & Aboud, 1981) that addresses the responsibilities of counselor education programs in meeting the objectives of Section 504 of the Vocational Rehabilitation Act of 1973: To prohibit discrimination against all handicapped individuals attempting to participate in any program or activity that receives federal financial assistance. This article speaks not to the content of counselor education programs but to their accessibility to handicapped persons, particularly regarding admissions criteria and elimination of physical barriers.

It seems apparent that if one were to sum up the current state of priorities in content and supervised experiences in counselor education, emphases on working with exceptional persons as defined by learning disabilities, cognitive and physical handicaps, or speech and hearing disorders would not be the rule across the nation. Rather, counselor education programs would be directed to "normal" rather than "exceptional" populations. Beyond that it might be argued, as several observers do (Hansen & Tennyson, 1975; Hohenshil, 1979; Hohenshil & Ryan, 1977; Maples, 1978; McDaniels, 1978), that not only is there insufficient attention given in counselor training to working with exceptional persons, there is also insufficient attention given to career guidance and/or to career development as major counselor responsibilities. To the degree that these views are accurate, it is obvious that the conjunction of the two emphases, counselor training for career development of exceptional persons, occurs even *less* frequently than counselor training in exceptionalities or in more broadly conceived career guidance/career development.

CAREER DEVELOPMENT FOR EXCEPTIONAL PEOPLE

A review of the practices associated with facilitating the career development of exceptional persons can provide a base for extrapolating needed modifications in counselor training to accommodate exceptional persons.

With respect to vocational or career development itself, Hershenson (1974) contended that "Relatively little has been written on the vocational development of the handicapped," although he went on to point out that "the onset of a disability generally creates a discontinuity in career development, particularly if it occurs in mid-career" (pp. 486, 487).

Sinick (1979) indicated that

> Earlier discontinuities occur with earlier onsets. Many disabling conditions are congenital or arise early in life, whether from diseases, accidents or other life events. Young people with disabilities often progress slowly or disjointedly through their vocational stages. Impeding factors include reduced mobility, sensory or mental impairment, and prolonged medical treatment. Such factors make it difficult for affected persons to keep pace with their peers in career development. (p. 252)

Sinick went on to contend that handicapped young people may be expected to exhibit greater vocational aspiration-expectation differences as functions of distortions of body image and self-concept, overgeneralized feelings of inadequacy, overcompensatory mechanisms, dependence/independence dilemmas, family influences, and counselor misperceptions.

Savino, Belchick, and Brean (1971) have argued that the search for vocational implications of such conditions as paraplegia, quadriplegia, and other severely handicapping positions has only occurred in earnest since World War II. Until that time and as long as serious injuries and disabling conditions were considered catastrophic and resulted in profound disablement or death, vocational implication, vocational evaluations, and methods of work adjustment were not seen as particularly important emphases within rehabilitation.

Lassiter (1981) has suggested that newer techniques in physical medicine and in rehabilitation have caused the vocational needs of severely disabled persons to be given serious attention in counseling approaches to such populations. He proposed analyzing the vocational needs of handicapped populations within a Maslowian format, which recognizes that such needs are never independent of the physical, psychological, or social needs of people with severe physical limitations. He furthered his advocacy of counseling in response to the vocational implications of severe disabilities by citing the observation of Neff (1977) that "the problems of work behavior are, in large part at least, problems of personality."

Using Maslow's (1970) frame of reference and advances in techniques, Lassiter suggested the types of concepts and skills important to the counselor doing career development with severely disabled persons.

Physiological Needs

The basic physiological needs of the person who has suffered a traumatic injury or disabling condition are to survive, engage in a schedule of nutrition, fight infection with drug use, and undergo surgical procedures, muscle redevelopment, and reeducation. An adjunct to such conditions is the frequent need to teach the patient the basic physical survival skills or, more likely, teach new skills to accommodate the new physical limitations—new methods in self-care and mobility, activities of daily living. The major needs with significance for work and work adjustment in a competitive work setting are:

1. Need to learn to work in a wheelchair (e.g., using the bathroom, traveling from home to work, taking a coffee break, meeting with fellow workers, dealing with different job performance tasks at the workplace).
2. Need to learn new ways of being productive (e.g., coping with a work time schedule different from others, using specially structured pieces, instruments, or machines to enable the client to meet the job

demands, receiving an individualized instructional program in mobility).
3. Need for the client to accept responsibility for personal hygiene (e.g., attending to bathroom and other personal needs, learning to care well for his or her body and avoid the medical complications and illnesses that result in absenteeism, loss of productive activity, and more severe disablement).

Safety Needs

Here the client is concerned with security and stability, freedom from fear, anxiety, and chaos, and personal protection. The vocational needs implicit in safety include:
1. The strong desire on the part of the client to remain in work similar to a preferred previous job and a preference for association with familiar people on the job.
2. The need for a job that seems to offer greater tenure and stability with better-than-average health and retirement plans, etc.
3. The need for a smoothly functioning position with order clearly established.

Belongingness and Love Needs

For the first time in his or her life, the disabled person may "feel sharply the pangs of loneliness, of ostracism, of rejection, of friendlessness, or restlessness" (Maslow, 1970). Therefore, after physical and safety needs are met, the emphasis is on meeting the need for love and affection. If such needs are not or cannot be met on the job, the question for vocational planning becomes one of how to provide instruction and counseling that can help the client find new ways of developing feelings of belonging, participating in personal growth groups with nondisabled persons in the community, and analyzing the potential for caring and being cared for. These needs might be met in the job setting if certain job modifications or support groups were developed.

Esteem Needs

There is an opportunity in vocational planning and work adjustment to provide training programs for the client to develop skills necessary to meet the esteem needs (e.g., to experience new feelings of competence and self-confidence that come from a person's exposure to new interpersonal skills and new tasks). Such planning usually involves a variety of approaches including specific work task assignments, individual counseling and the use of small group sessions incorporating a combination of affective and cognitive activities, and the use of milieu therapy to engage the client in various social encounters.

Self-Actualization Needs

Techniques recommended by Lassiter to meet the self-actualization needs of people with severe disabilities include activities such as meditation, Gestalt awareness exercises, alpha feedback, and use of fantasies, daydreams, and other self-awareness exercises that can be provided either in individual or group counseling. Quoting Wax (1972), Lassiter presented four major reasons for assisting seriously handicapped people in a self-awareness and self-actualization program: (1) A rich inner life may make being alone less painful. (2) Inner space (or thought) may be the only area left for a feeling of freedom and autonomy for those who are dependent on others. (3) Effective use of this inner space (being happy with your thoughts and feelings) offers an alternative to the hyperactivity of people who fear depression or existential despair. (4) Solitude and the ability to think and ask ourselves the hard questions give us the opportunity to develop a philosophy that helps us to live what must be lived (e.g., a life of severe disability).

Against this brief context, it seems appropriate to contend that counselors dealing with career development of exceptional persons must first know about models of career development across the life stages (see, e.g., Super, 1957). Beyond such awareness, however, they must recognize the characteristic patterns of discontinuity that accompany disability at various points of career development (Gribbons & Lohnes, 1968; Lo Cascio, 1964). Observed patterns of discontinuity must be viewed against the deficits in visual, hearing, dexterity, emotional performance occasioned by particular disabilities, the nature and extent of schooling, family perspectives, and influences or other cultural factors affecting career development of the individual. In addition to understanding methods of modifying arrested or impaired career development, counselors must also know how to relate the actual functional limitations imposed by medical or other "exceptional" conditions to job or to training demands rather than be guided by stereotypical generalities.

Sensitivities to the potential effects of particular disabilities experienced in different life stages should also modify the way counselors approach individual assessment, occupational information and exploration, counseling, placement, and follow-through. Thus, "generalist" counselor training needs to reflect attitudes, knowledge, and skills specially directed to the needs of exceptional persons.

Speaking specifically to counselors who work with spinal cord-injured clients, Hendrick (1981) stated that "In addition to general counseling skills, the counselor needs to be able to realistically evaluate the patient's alternatives for work or education, and must also know the current labor market as well as government resources that offer financial aid to spinal cord injured persons during vocational readjustment." In addition, she suggested that it is important to know about and be able to act on how various factors extrinsic to the patients themselves (e.g., institutional barriers, discriminatory hiring, disability payments as incentives to remain unemployed) combine with intrinsic factors (e.g., intelligence, previous work experiences, education) to delay reemployment.

Sinick (1979) has written about how standard career counselor practices need to be adapted to the particular needs of handicapped persons. For example, in his recommendations about testing, he cautioned that "individuals without much exposure to common experiences in the outside world often relate poorly to tests." He therefore advocated individual rather than group testing, using timed tests with caution, the need for rest periods and multiple sessions, awareness that visual, hearing, or other impairments can cause significant disparities across aptitude or intelligence test scores, and the fact that work samples (tests with face validity) have advantages over other types of tests. With respect to content information, Sinick argued that it is likely that persons deprived of life experiences will be unfamiliar with the content of many common interest inventories. Therefore, the direct use of the interview to discuss interests, values, needs, and goals rather than more indirect methods of obtaining such information is generally warranted.

Rather than using primarily abstract occupational information (pamphlets, directories, booklets), Sinick contended that such information is better obtained directly from work sites where handicapped clients can gain direct information about general knowledge of work, the community's geography and transportation, as well as the more specific likelihood about the way work sites do or do not adapt to functional limitations of various kinds. He further argued that each of these aspects of career counseling must be supported by the counselor's ongoing attention to enhancing the client's self-esteem and to the likelihood that the clients will need very specific attention to placement readiness and employment readiness: job-seeking and job-finding skills.

Brolin and Gysbers (1979) have discussed the importance of providing career education for persons with handicaps. They advocated focusing career education on assisting individuals to develop critical life skills essential for successful living and working. They suggested that such programs be organized around competencies that handicapped individuals need to acquire for successful career development. These competencies can, in turn, be divided into three categories of concern: daily living, personal-social, and occupational.

RECOMMENDATIONS ON COUNSELOR TRAINING FOR CAREER DEVELOPMENT FOR EXCEPTIONAL PERSONS

The previous sections of this chapter identify attitudinal and content dimensions that need to be included in counselor training for career development for exceptional persons. Although not exhaustive, they represent points of reference regarding potential categories of knowledge or skills that might be included in counselor training.

Perhaps overriding information or even skills in their importance, however, is the challenge for counselors in training to deal with their attitudes toward the disabled. They need to examine and act upon their comfort in working with persons who have experienced different handicapping conditions, their stereotypes about the spread or generalizability of such conditions to other aspects of the person's life, and the effects of labeling or stigmata that handicapped persons are likely to have incorporated into their self-concept and their behavior. Counselor attitude toward the disabled must be examined through multiple training opportunities (e.g., role playing the effects of handicapping conditions, observing handicapped persons in various work and social circumstances, viewing films and other visual recordings of behavioral adjustments that can be made to compensate for "exceptional" circumstances, and direct relationships with exceptional persons either as a supervised counselor of such persons or as colleagues/friends in counselor education).

Beyond this matter of attitude toward exceptional persons who have experienced various handicapping conditions and who are therefore likely to be exposed to different stimuli or to act upon such stimuli differently than "normal persons," counselors dealing with the career development of exceptional persons need other types of knowledge and skills. Much of this knowledge and many of these skills will have to be developed carefully with the help and advice of other professionals who work with the handicapped.

REFERENCES

Bell, H. A. (1962). Attitudes of selected rehabilitation workers and other hospital employees toward the physically disabled. *Psychological Reports*, *10*, 183–186.

Brolin, D. E., & Gysbers, N. C. (1979). Career education for persons with handicaps. *Personnel and Guidance Journal, 58*(4), 258–262.

Fix, C., & Rohrbacker, J. (1977). What is a handicap? The impact of attitudes. *Personnel and Guidance Journal, 56*(3), 176–178.

Gribbons, W., & Lohnes, P. (1968). *Emerging careers.* New York: Teachers College Press.

Hansen, L. S., & Tennyson, W. W. (1975). A career management model for counselor involvement. *Personnel and Guidance Journal, 53,* 638–645.

Hendrick, S. S. (1981). Spinal cord injury: A special kind of loss. *Personnel and Guidance Journal, 59*(6), 355–359.

Hershenson, D. B. (1974). Vocational guidance and the handicapped. In E. L. Herr (Ed.), *Vocational guidance and human development.* Boston: Houghton Mifflin.

Hohenshil, T. H. (1979). Renewal in career guidance and counseling: Rationale and programs. *Counselor Education and Supervision, 18*(3), 199–207.

Hohenshil, T. H., & Ryan, C. W. (1977). Continuing professional development in career education. *American Vocational Journal, 52*(3), 40–42.

Hosie, T. W. (1979). Preparing counselors to meet the needs of the handicapped. *Personnel and Guidance Journal, 58*(4), 271–275.

Humes, C. W. (1978). Implications of P.L. 94-142 for training and supervision. *Counselor Education and Supervision, 18*(2), 126–129.

Ibrahim, F., & Herr, E. L. (1982). Attitude modification toward disability: Differential effect of two educational modes. *Rehabilitation Counseling Bulletin, 26,* 29–36.

Ioracchini, E. V., & Aboud, R. R. (1981). A look at counselor education programs in light of Section 504 of the Rehabilitation Act of 1973. *Counselor Education and Supervision, 21*(2), 109–118.

Lamy, R. E. (1966). Social consequences of mental illness. *Journal of Consulting Psychology, 30,* 450–455.

Lassiter, R. A. (1981). *Work evaluation and work adjustment for severely handicapped people, a counseling approach.* Paper presented at International Round Table for the Advancement of Counselling Consultation on Career Guidance and Higher Education, Cambridge, England, December 13–18.

Lo Cascio, R. (1964). Delayed and impaired vocational development: A neglected aspect of vocational development theory. *Personnel and Guidance Journal, 42,* 885–887.

Lombana, J. H. (1980). Guidance of handicapped students: Counselor in-service needs. *Counselor Education and Supervision, 19*(4), 269–275.

Maples, M. (1978). Facilitators and barriers in the practice of guidance and counseling. In *The status of guidance and counseling in the nation's schools.* Washington, DC: American Personnel and Guidance Association.

Maslow, A. H. (1970). *Motivation and personality* (2nd ed.). New York: Harper & Row.

McDaniels, C. O. (1978). The practice of career guidance and counseling. In *The status of guidance and counseling in the schools.* Washington, DC: American Personnel and Guidance Association.

Neff, W. (1977). *Work and human behavior* (2nd ed.). Chicago: Aldine.

Pederson, P., Holwill, C. F., & Shapiro, J. (1978). A cross-cultural training procedure for classes in counselor education. *Counselor Education and Supervision, 17*(3), 233–237.

Savino, M., Belchick, J., & Brean, E. (1971). Quadriplegics in a university setting. *Rehabilitation Record, November-December, 12,* 3–9.

Sinick, D. (1979). Career counseling with handicapped persons. *Personnel and Guidance Journal, 58*(4), 252–257.

Super, D. E. (1957). *The psychology of careers*. New York: Harper.

Tringo, J. L. (1968). *The hierarchy of preference: A comparison of attitudes and prejudices toward specific disability groups*. Unpublished doctoral dissertation, University of Connecticut, Storrs.

Vandergriff, A. F., & Hosie, T. W. (1979). P.L. 94-142: A role change of counselors or just an extension of present role? *Journal of Counseling Services, 3*(1), 6–11.

Vontress, C. E. (1970). Counseling blacks. *Personnel and Guidance Journal, 48,* 713–719.

Wax, J. (1972). The inner life, a new dimension of rehabilitation. *Journal of Rehabilitation, 38,* 16–18.

Conclusion

Nancy M. Pinson-Millburn

The primary intent of this text is to sample current educational thinking and endeavor in what is still a virgin industry: one in which machines and people are successfully collaborating in behalf of the handicapped populations of this nation. To a commendable degree, this partnership has begun to take on form and substance, despite its pioneering status among helping professionals.

Educators first became intrigued with the computer's potential back in the 1950s (Karoff, 1983), well after the first electronic digital computer (ENIAC) was erected at the University of Pennsylvania in 1946. But exploration of a possible merger between counseling and high technology began in earnest only 20 years ago. In *Computer-Assisted Guidance*, Super (1970) and his colleagues recorded such initiatives as dating from 1964. Although none of these early efforts linked computers, career development, and the handicapped, computer-assisted guidance has enjoyed professional attention since the advent of one of its first systems, Educational and Career Exploration (ECES).

Rehabilitation counselors have also recognized the importance of preparing themselves for the computer age (Goodman, 1981; Lofaro, 1983; McGuire, 1981; Myers, 1980; Nagy & Donald, 1981). Nave and Browning (1983) made particular reference to the importance of computer literacy to the helping professions by noting several valuable resources. Among them are: (1) a special issue of *Computer* (January 1981) dedicated to the handicapped; (2) the Apple Clearinghouse for the Handicapped's production of many useful materials, including "Personal Computing for the Physically Disabled"; (3) a focus on computer technology in state vocational rehabilitation agencies in the Institute on Rehabilitation's 8th Report; and (4) a reference to the Johns Hopkins Applied Physics Laboratory's national search for innovative applications of personal computing that could aid the handicapped; a key stimulus for the colloquium guiding this text.

Engineers, particularly mechanical and rehabilitation engineers, have led the professions in embracing medicine, engineering, and related sciences as they apply technology to the needs of the disabled. O'Reagan (1983) provided a comprehensive summary of their accomplishments in his monograph entitled "Rehabilitation Technology in the 1980's." Communications technology is the subject of much of his discussion, and he reported that the Institute of Electronic and Electrical Engineers has established a special committee to study the application of micro-computers and microprocessors to the functioning of the disabled.

The lay press, representing an unusually well-informed public perception of our potential allies in this challenge, has been equally outspoken on the capacitating qualities of computers. The *Wall Street Journal* (Experiments May Eventually Help," 1983) provided an in-depth follow-up to *Time* magazine's article "Power to the Disabled" (Faflick, 1982). Both sources celebrated the moment when a paralyzed woman walked under the control of a computer firing commands to her helpless legs. Their reports noted that the 500,000 Americans now suffering from paralysis of two or more limbs could rightfully anticipate the streamlining and miniaturization of current devices to the degree that they could one day be implanted as pacemakers now are. They further observed that certain voice-activated input devices can be taught more than 40 commands and are already being used by quadriplegics.

Arnold Packer (1983) of the *Washington Post* believed that not only can computers reduce illiteracy among the 25 million Americans who cannot read or write, but that they can also improve the work skills of 72 million who are functionally illiterate, including 30 million foreign-born Americans whose command of English is poor to nonexistent. Packer also sees the computer offering essential mental stimulation to the institu-tionalized elderly.

Karoff (1983), an education reporter for the same newspaper, noted that 58% of our schools today have at least one terminal (one for every 400 students) and that if the current trend continues, at least 40% of all microcomputer sales will be to school systems by 1986. He expressed some alarm, however, over the rapidity with which schools are installing microcomputers without considering quality programming.

This concern is echoed in *Time* magazine's "Machine of the Year" issue (Friederich, 1983) where there is ample corroboration for both the promise and continued challenge of the computer, particularly for the handicapped. Despite its advances in measuring living functions, speci-fying insulin requirements, stimulating deadened muscles, and translating sound into vibrations, *Time*'s reporters agreed that only 20% of the currently available software has achieved the necessary quality to warrant widespread distribution.

Given the ingredients of collaboration and the exciting potential of new alliances, it is appropriate to question the ability of educators and counselors to engage these challenges. Previously, counselors were trained to view all people as "exceptional" or "special," thus blurring both the service and commitment lines that tend to be drawn by society as a whole when it distinguishes between groups. Although this diffusion may increase acceptance of differences, it may also remove or displace responsibility.

We must recognize that discontinuity of career development is more likely to characterize the handicapped as they mature chronologically and physically. New career development theories are critically needed to accommodate the handicapped. These theories must view the unconventional and multiple trial aspects of so-called normal career development stages as particularly relevant for these populations.

Furthermore, these theories must be translated into practice. Counselors and educators working together and assisted by computer and other information-age technology can be a major force in providing a better life for many handicapped individuals previously deprived of careers.

The application of technology to the handicapped, particularly in the area of career development, makes several important assumptions: 1) that those involved with career development will resist the tendency to become the purview of a single group of professionals; 2) that those involved with career development will maintain a rigorously objective and nonpolitical perspective on the rights of future beneficiaries; and 3) that these clients, their families, and their employers will be continuously involved in the selection and testing of new systems.

As Arias (1981) has observed, the future of computerized communication aids will be comparable to the history of the automobile: Everyone will be fascinated and more than a few will wish to become involved. Soon there will be devices that some handicapped persons can purchase and to some extent customize themselves, thus obviating the need for a professional intermediary. But other persons will continue to need the assistance of trained practitioners with systems and programs that will one day be mass-produced at far lower cost.

The charge to professionals is straightforward. Because technological and scientific discovery will continue, with or without their consent, their power lies in an extraordinary capacity to direct and enrich those advances in such a way that the less fortunate among us are the first to benefit.

REFERENCES

Arias, R. (1981). Computer communication devices for the handicapped. *Rx Home Care*, *3*(7), 51–56.
Experiments may eventually help some paraplegics to walk. *Wall Street Journal*, April 15, 1983, p. 33.

Faflick, P. (1982, December 13). Power to the disabled. *Time*, pp. 76–82.

Friederich, O. (1983, January 3). The computer moves in. *Time*, pp. 14–24.

Goodman, S. M. (1981). A study to determine changes in time utilization, autonomy and correlated work-ready attitudes in a heterogeneous population of disabled individuals learning computer programming (doctoral dissertation, University of Cincinnati, 1980). *Dissertation Abstracts International, 41,* 2760B–2761B.

Karoff, P. (1983). Computers: Too much too soon. *The Washington Post Summer Education Review*, April 17.

Lofaro, G. A. (1983). 1981 annual dissertation review: An annotated bibliography. *Rehabilitation Counseling Bulletin, 26*(3), 185–203.

McGuire, G. M. (1981). The development of a computer-assisted vocational guidance system for use in rehabilitation counseling (doctoral dissertation, West Virginia University, 1981). *Dissertation Abstracts International, 42,* 1012A.

Myers, J. (1980). Counseling the disabled older person for the world of work. *Journal of Employment Counseling, 17*(1), 37–48.

Nagy, D. R., & Donald, G. M. (1981). Computerized career guidance systems and beyond. In D. H. Montross and C. J. Shinkman (Eds.), *Career development in the 1980's: Theory and practice*. Springfield, IL: Charles C Thomas.

Nave, G., & Browning, P. (1983). Preparing rehabilitation leaders for the computer age. *Rehabilitation Counseling Bulletin, 26*(5), 364–367.

O'Reagan, J. (1983). Rehabilitation technology in the 1980s. In S. Sellars (Ed.), *Futures Symposium*. College Park, MD: Center of Rehabilitation and Manpower Services, University of Maryland.

Packer, A. (1983). The good computers could do. *The Washington Post*, Op-Ed, January 6.

Super, D. E. (1970). *Computer-assisted counseling*. New York: Teachers College Press.

Tesolowski, D. G., & Halpin, G. (1979). Modifying work personalities of the handicapped. *Vocational Guidance Quarterly, 27*(4), 334–340.

Resource Guide to Computer Technology and the Handicapped

Lynn Rogers

The review of the literature on computer assistance to the career development for the handicapped calls attention to and confirms the fact that, to date, these component fields remain basically separate from each other. Because so little has been published in the area of career-focused technology for the handicapped, available publications have been classified as those which address technological aids for the handicapped, technological aids for career development, and career development for the handicapped.

The code next to each annotation indicates which disciplines are combined in the particular reference. The letter C indicates a computer technology emphasis, the letter H addresses the handicapped, and the letter V (for vocation, to distinguish it from computers) indicates a career development component. Therefore, the code C/H/V, found only three times in this search, indicates that the publication being referenced includes components of computer technology, services to handicapped, and career development. The code C/H, with the largest number of references found (42), refers to references that address computer technology aids for handicapped, while C/V (7 references found) refers to computer technology aids in career development; H/V showing the second largest number of references (32), addresses career development for handicapped (handicapped vocations). Computer technology aids for the handicapped are divided unequally in the literature between educational aids and functional aids, with a majority dealing with educational aids. The 32 references related to career development of the handicapped also showed a leaning toward vocational programs within the educational system.

Our reference to handicapped persons includes physical, mental, and emotional disability. Career development refers primarily to income-producing activity within the range of potential and interest of the individual, although in some instances life-style and maximum potential functioning are also considered. Technological aids refer to computer-based assistance. Young people seem to be highly favored in consideration for services in the frequency of reports.

The journals that reported relevant research in the professional fields identified were given preference. Computer searches were made through ERIC, Psychological Abstracts, Sociological Abstracts, and National Clearing House for Mental Health. Nineteen eighty-three issues of these and other related periodicals, including computer periodicals, were searched individually. Dissertation abstracts were included. A list of the periodicals consulted appears after the annotated bibliography.

In addition to selections from periodical literature included in the sample, readers will note that this is followed by special attention paid to selected publications and institutional resources. We also want to acknowledge the excellent sources provided by James R. O'Reagan in his paper "Rehabilitation Technology in the 1980's." That article was one of several included in *Future Symposium*, published by the Center of Rehabilitation and Manpower Services, the University of Maryland, College Park, in 1983.

The traditional policy has been to emphasize vocational services, separate from and often in opposition to career development, for handicapped persons. We now have an opportunity, by joining the disciplines with the benefits of computer technology aids, to creatively expand this service to career development and maximum potential life-style functioning services for the handicapped. The pertinence of conducting a literature review at this time rests on the opportunity to discover what has been learned in these fields prior to the deliberate joining of the disciplines for creative career development services for this population.

C/H   Ayers, G. E. The learner and the computer. Paper presented at the National Conference on Computer-Based Education, Bloomington, Minnesota, October 1980.

The problems of declining student enrollment at the secondary level and changes in the types of learners served is addressed by computer-based instruction for such learners as the disadvantaged, part-time students, the handicapped, and school dropouts. Useful and timely instruction for these groups is presented by such projects as PLATO and TICCIT, with the expectation that these groups will continue to comprise a growing segment of our population. Developmental skills as well as more complex models of simulation, inquiry, and dialogue are presented for use by these special populations, as well as special input and output devices designed to increase their communication skills. The motivation of these students is one of the prime targets of the computer-based instruction programs.

H/V   Bingham, G. Career maturity of learning disabled adolescents. *Psychology in the Schools*, 1980, *17*(1), 135–139.

Bingham used Crites' Career Maturity Inventory to assess the career maturity of 32 students attending a private high school for students with learning disabilities. She compared the results from this sample to those of a sample of 30, each learning and non-learning-disabled public high school students from her 1978 study (in which she had given only the Attitude Scale of the CMI), and to Crites' reported mean scores for each subtest of the Competence Test of the CMI. She found that: 1) there were no differences between the public and private learning disabled students in career attitudes; 2) there was a significant difference between private school learning-disabled and public school non-learning-disabled students in career attitudes; and 3) there were no significant differences in scores on the Competence Test between the learning-disabled students and Crites' reported means. Values, attitudes, and feelings need to be addressed in career guidance of the learning disabled.

H/V   Bordel, R. Preparing physically handicapped adolescents for their integration into vocational training and gainful employment. *International Journal of Rehabilitation Research*, 1981, *4*(4), 541–542.

This report of the development of a program for physically handicapped youth in West Germany, grades 7–9, details the use of films, role-playing, and teacher commentaries to improve the students' knowledge and understanding of career choices, vocational adjustment, legislation concerning young handicapped people, and social behavior.

C/H   Brebner, A., & Hallworth, H. J. A multi-media CAI Terminal based upon a microprocessor with application for the handicapped. Paper presented at the Annual Conference of the Association for Educational Data Systems, St. Louis, Missouri, April 1980.

The author presents three basic requirements for providing appropriate instruction to the developmentally handicapped by means of computer-assisted instruction: probability, reliability, and flexibility. If the system meets these requirements, it is suitable for the customary learning environment, is a reliable teaching and learning tool, and can make use of new input and output devices as they become available. Special features mentioned are double-sized characters, graphic characters, color, animation, synthetic speech, and control of a slide projector. Cerebral palsied students can also make use of the POSSUM apparatus and the POSSUM expanded keyboard, which allow for easier student response.

H/V   Brody-Hasazi, S., Salembier, G., & Finck, K. Directions for the 80's: Vocational preparation for secondary mildly handicapped students. *Teaching Exceptional Children*, 1983, 15(4), 206–209.

A secondary school model teaching mildly handicapped students the skills needed for locating, securing, and maintaining employment is presented in this paper. Emphasis is placed on inclusion of skills necessary to function effectively and appropriately in the community, and the necessity of cooperation between special and vocational educators in planning and implementing a program. Assessment procedures, support services, work experiences, securing of employment, and follow-up and transitional services are included in student objectives; flexible teacher schedules, systematic follow-up procedure, and identification of handicapped students in need of services are included in program objectives.

H/V   Brolin, E., & Carver, J. T. Lifelong career development for adults with handicaps: A new model. *Journal of Career Education*, 1982, 8(4), 280–292.

Lifelong career development for the handicapped is defined as the optimal degree of independent functioning and includes skills of daily living and self-care, personal and social interaction skills, and specific occupational skills. This program, developed and reported by the authors, approaches the acquisition of these skills in a systematic manner, with the goal of developing these skills for future as well as current use.

C/H   Budoff, M., & Hutten, L. R. Microcomputers in special education: Promises and pitfalls. *Exceptional Children*, 1982, 49(2), 123–128.

Microcomputer systems that serve special education are described here, including their major features, limitations of their use for special education students, and questions of their effectiveness for this population. The necessity of teachers to

become knowledgeable about and comfortable with the systems
and software is stressed.

H/V   Canedo, A. R. A structured work program for physically
disabled youth: Its effects on various aspects of vocational
development and personality. Temple University, Philadelphia 1980. (Order #8025121)

The study was composed around often-asked the question of
whether or not and how a work experience program may affect
the personal maturity and ability to enter the world of work of
physically disabled youth. The author engaged physically
disabled youth in such a program for 8 weeks, and compared
them in terms of personal/social growth and vocational maturity
with disabled youth who had not participated in the work
experience. Self-evaluative tests given to all subjects during the
last week of the program revealed that the experimental subjects
scored higher in attitudes toward disabilities, ego strength,
ability to bind anxiety, and career maturity, the largest differences being in the first two areas noted. Sex differentiation
showed males to score higher in ego strength, whereas females
scored higher in attitudes toward disabilities. The results support
the effective use of work experience programs to increase the
personal growth and career maturity of physically disabled
youth.

C/H   Chaffin, J. D. et al. ARC-ED curriculum: the application of
video game formats to educational software. *Exceptional
Children*, 1982, *49*(2), 173–178.

ARC-ED Curriculum is the name suggested for a proposed
educational program for exceptional children based on video
arcade game formats. Educational microcomputer software
applicability for this use is explored, with guidelines for the
development of the educational curriculum.

H/V   Clark, G. Handicapped adolescents: A matter of appropriate
education. *Exceptional Education Quarterly*, 1980, *1*,
11–17,

The need for formal education to incorporate career education in
an individualized way for the handicapped is addressed in this
article, "career" being defined as "the course of one's life" with
emphasis on work. Occupational development, daily living
skills, personal-social skills, and career preparation for the
handicapped are presented with research evidence and offered
as essentials of formal education at the secondary level. The

appropriateness of an educational program that does not completely cover these areas is strongly questioned.

H/V   Cobb, R. A curriculum-based approach to vocational assessment. *Teaching Exceptional Children*, 1983, 15(4), 216–219.

Assessment procedures for provision of vocational curricula for handicapped students are presented and described, including screening, placement, program planning, assessment of individual progress, and program evaluation. It brings vocational assessment back to the classroom and encourages informal, continuous classroom-based assessments.

C/H   "Computer Assisted Research and Instruction for the Hearing Impaired National Conference—Symposium on Research and Utilization of Educational Media for Teaching the Deaf", *American Annals for the Deaf*, September 1983, Vol. 128, No. 5, Pgs. 511–774 (entire edition)

This issue is devoted to the topic of microcomputers in education of the hearing impaired taking its papers from the Symposium on Research and Utilization of Educational Media for Teaching the Deaf. The National Conference, sponsored by Captioned Films and Telecommunications Branch, Division of Educational Services, Office of Special Education and Educational Media Production Project for the Hearing Impaired—Barkley Memorial Center, the University of Nebraska—Lincoln Teachers College, presents the 34 papers on the topic presented at the Symposium. Vocational assessment is viewed as a matching of curriculum, student, and training environment. The writer asserts that "Program planning for handicapped students should be based primarily upon achievement testing of observable skills, and much less upon interest and aptitude testing of inherent qualities." Vocational assessment is delineated from vocational evaluation, and presented as an attempt to "match curriculum, student, and training environment" in an effort to more efficiently aid the handicapped in obtaining vocational knowledge and experience during their school years.

C/H   *Computing Teacher*. What can the computer and the YPLA do for handicapped children? 1982, *November*, 36.

This brief article introduces the voice recognition aptitude of computers, which will allow handicapped individuals who are unable to talk clearly make some sound or movement that the computer will translate to specific words. Examples are given of use of the Scott Instruments Shadow/Vet system, Apple Logo vocabularies, Type 'N Talk synthetic speech, and the prospect of developing a synthetic speech system that will hook up to a computer.

C/V D'Abrosca, L. A., & Sink, C. V. Microcomputers in business education. *Journal of Business Education*, 1982, *58*(2), 47–49.

The basics of computer literacy, including data and word processing, text editing, keyboarding, file organization, and basic mathematics, are presented here as being taught within a business education program with the use of microcomputers.

H/V Dahl, R. Maximizing vocational opportunities for handicapped clients. *Vocational Guidance Quarterly*, 1982, 31(1), 43–52.

The author presents a broad picture of vocational programs for the handicapped and barriers to employment with ways to overcome the barriers, and identifies occupations in which severely handicapped persons successfully perform. Barriers mentioned include unrealistic expectations and attitudes, as well as inadequate skills.

C/H Debonis, D. M. et al. Education's new alphabet: Alphanumeric, byte, chip. *Academic Therapy*, 1982, *18*(2), 133–140.

The Farrell Middle School in Farrell, Pennsylvania, devised a computer-assisted project to improve students' skills in math, particularly computation, concept development, problem solving, and application of mathematical concepts. Interestingly, the program was believed to be suitable for a wide variety of exceptional students from fifth to eighth grades, including learning-disabled, mildly mentally retarded, severely mentally retarded, and gifted students.

C/V Dianni-Surridge, M. Technology and work: Future issues for career guidance. *The Personnel and Guidance Journal*, 1983, *61*(7), 413–416.

This article focuses on occupational structure changes resulting from advances in communication and microcomputer technologies and the possible resulting consequences for career guidance professionals.

C/V Edelstein, M. R. The use of a microcomputer as an aide in career exploration. Dissertation paper, Texas A & M University, College Station, December 1982.

This study was designed to test the use of a microcomputer as a method of presenting career information. Holland's Self Directed Search was used with three groups: one using a paper-and-pencil version, one using a computerized version, and one using expanded computerized versions. All received a counseling session after the SDS was completed in addition to the Career Interest Survey and a student questionnaire. It was expected that those taking the computerized SDS would show either more crystallized interests or expanded career options. This was not the case. Possible explanations for the lack of significance are presented.

H/V   Ellington, C. Career education: People and programs working together. *Teaching Exceptional Children*, 1983, *15*(4), 210–215.

The need for cooperative efforts of parents, teachers, students, guidance counselors, occupational specialists, work experience teachers, and the vocational education community is presented as the key to provision of career education for handicapped and disadvantaged students. Roles of the different team members are described, as well as development of cooperative resources if these personnel are not available.

H/V   Ellington, C., & Winkoff, L. Low cost implementation of a career education program for elementary school children with handicaps. *Journal of Career Education*, 1982, *8*(4), 246–255.

Two programs that use existing school resources and are extremely low cost are presented. Each deals with the problem of career education of handicapped children. One is an integration of career education with academic education, whereas the other provides opportunity for the children to try out and experience different work settings and tasks.

C/H   Faflick, P. Power to the disabled. *Time*, December 13, 1982, *120*, 76.

Specialized, unusual individual use of computer aids are described in the cases of two severely handicapped young people. The brother of a quadriplegic has put together computerized voice-control equipment that allows the disabled man to order the computer to make a satellite search and hook him in to any one of 150 TV channels, dial the telephone, adjust the angle of his bed, dim the lights, dictate letters, play video games, and write computer programs. They are working on a robot arm for the patient. The second case is a young woman paralyzed below the rib cage. She was able to take several steps recently with the aid of a very cumbersome system that combines electrical stimulation techniques and modern high-speed computers. The system, and plans for perfecting it and its uses, are described.

H/V   Fair, G. W., & Sullivan, A. R. Career opportunities for culturally diverse handicapped youth. *Exceptional Children*, 1980, *46*(8), 626–631.

Vocational achievement of this group is investigated and an overview of the findings presented. The barriers to this group in achieving successful employment are reported, including architectural barriers, ideological differences, the sometimes complicated process of becoming employable, and individual affective problems that present barriers to employment. Provision of a positive, encouraging atmosphere and recognition and accommodation of individual differences are cited as aids in allowing for success of this population.

C/H/V   Flanigan, D. *Computerized aide for the handicapped*. Washington, D.C.: National Institute of Education, September 1981.

Uses of the computer to aid the handicapped are presented. Included in aids to education and employment are simulation of laboratory experiments, remedial instruction, the use of the computer in the worker's home, and computer programming as a career for the handicapped. Individuals with visual handicaps, communication disabilities, and other disabilities make use of a variety of computerized aids and devices addressing many life problems; devices considered include talking meters, braille terminals, standard print readers, auditory adjuncts, diagnostic and therapy aids, wheelchairs, environmental control devices, worktables, self-feeding devices, scanners and direct selection types of communication aids, as well as those mentioned which aid in career development. Recent improvements in computer applications, as well as weaknesses or current technology, are identified.

H/V   Fonosch, G. C., Aranz, J., Lee, A., & Loving, S. Providing career planning and placement services for college students with disabilities. *Exceptional Education Quarterly*, 1982, *3*(3), 67–74.

A program designed to provide career development services for disabled college students is presented here to illustrate the special career development needs of disabled students and how these needs can be met. Specific needs of this population in career development are described, as well as the need to focus on identification of these needs, continuing removal of architectural barriers, the training of staff to aid disabled students, and continuing research and experimentation to develop more effective programs and approaches. Section 504 Rehabilitation

Act of 1973 is a focal point to emphasize cooperative efforts for delivery of services.

H/V   Gannaway, T. W., Sink, J. M., & Becket, W. C. A predictive validity study of a job sample program with handicapped and disadvantaged individuals. *Vocational Guidance Quarterly*, 1980, *29*(1), 4–11.

An evaluation tool titled Vocational Evaluation System was used to predict job retention among 55 handicapped and 70 disadvantaged clients. Results of testing the tool indicate that its use by counselors will permit the counselor greater confidence in guidance of individuals toward specific occupations.

C/V   Garis, J. W. The integration of a computer-based guidance system in a college counseling center: A comparison of the effects of "discover" and individual counseling upon career planning. Dissertation paper, March 1983. Pennsylvania State University, State College, Pa.

The study was designed to test the effects on career planning in the use of DISCOVER Computer-Based Career Guidance and Counselor Support System versus individual career counseling. The three treatments were DISCOVER, individual career counseling, and a combination of the two. Results were as follows: All treatments produced positive effects, and each treatment alone was equivalent in positive influence. DISCOVER resulted in greater career library use, whereas career counseling stimulated more resource contacts. Treatments did not affect decision making or occupational knowledge, and use of both treatments was more effective than use of either alone.

C/H   Garr, D. Computereyes. *Science Digest*, 1983, *91*, 68.

Three new computer aids for the handicapped now being tested are described. The first is a seeing-eye computer. This is a camera that fits over the ear and sends pictures of any potential hazard within 20 feet to a microcomputer, which verbally identifies the hazard. The direction of the hazard is located by stereophonic sound and a tapping on the forehead signals the number of feet away. The system is currently cumbersome, but thought possible to be miniaturized for convenient use. Also for the blind, devices have been implanted in the visual cortexes of several blind volunteers that contain as many as 64 electrodes that stimulate the brain when a TV camera translates an image by computer into electrical pulses. This is an early stage of development, with a goal of perfecting a miniature TV camera that fits into a glass eye with the computer mounted in the eyeglass frames and as many as 512 electrodes linked to the brain. The third aid described allows a quadriplegic or individual with paralyzed hands to successfully order their hands to perform some functions. The command is given by shoulder or neck movements to a computer-based stimulator which stimulates hand muscles as ordered. Research proceeds with the goal of making the system implantable.

H/V   Gillet, P. It's elementary! Career education activities for mildly handicapped students. *Teaching Exceptional Children*, 1983, *15*(4), 197–205.

Incidental instruction and "infusion technique" are presented as planned instructional techniques in teaching career education to the mildly handicapped to be implemented in conjunction with incidental learning experiences and activities that relate academics to jobs and aspects of daily living. Emphasis is placed on the continuation of career education from elementary years through maturity, using academic skills, character training, social perception training, and relations of activities to careers and the world of work.

H/V   Gobble, E. M. R. A description of attitudes, interests, and knowledge about careers and selected personality characteristics in a group of spina bifida adolescents. Dissertation paper, University of Pittsburgh, 1980. (Order #8112672)

Through use of a battery of tests designed to indicate attitudes and knowledge about careers, perception of self-concept, and perception of personal control in the environment, a sample of 21 adolescents with spina bifida was evaluated in these areas separately as well as interactively. Career decision-making attitudes were at a less mature level among spina bifida patients than among the normative control group, and no significant differences between the groups were found in the areas of career knowledge, self-concept, and perception of control. Severity of disability did not affect career maturity or personal control in the environment, although more severely involved patients did indicate a more negative self-concept. Perception of self-concept was found to significantly affect perception of ability to work and career knowledge, whereas perception of control was an important factor affecting career decision-making attitudes and knowledge. Recommendations for further study and career education programs were made.

C/H   Goldenberg, E. P. *Special technology for special children: Computers to serve communication and autonomy in the education of handicapped children*. Austin: PRO-ED, 1979.

The field of artificial intelligence is approached for inter-disciplinary use by psychologists, educators, rehabilitation professionals, and scientists, with an eye toward helping these various specialists share their insights and work together. In four sections, the book addresses: 1) a philosophy of education for handicapped children and the role computers play in the education; 2) issues of computer-based educational environments and aids for physically handicapped, deaf, and autistic children, focusing on the handicaps themselves and issues of psychology and education of these three groups; 3) computer hardware and software and the technologies that have yet to be brought together to more effectively serve the handicapped; and 4) summary of research issues.

C/H   Grady, M. T. Long-range planning for computer use. *Educational Leadership*, 1983, *40*(8), 16–19.

The author addresses long-range planning of computer use in the microcomputer revolution in terms of remedial, gifted and talented, and general population students and the teaching of language arts, math, science, social studies, basic skills, and computer science. Target populations for the first year would be remedial and all students in the subjects of language arts, math, and computer literacy; general population in the subjects of language arts, math, science, social studies, and basic skills; in the second year, gifted and talented in the subjects of science and math the second year; and in the third year, general population in the subject of computer science and remedial population in the subjects of language arts and math.

C/H   Grimes, L. Computers are for kids: Designing software programs to avoid problems of learning. *Teaching Exceptional Children*, 1981, *14*(2), 49–53.

Handicapped students, particularly the learning disabled, are presented with special problems in selective attention, visual discrimination, reaction time, short-term memory, transferring and generalizing knowledge or information, recognition of mistakes, and social skills. The author proposed that computer-based instruction is effective in helping to overcome these deficits, and that the mastery of these problems and academic skills improves the student's self-concept. She provides a practical guide for teachers to develop and/or modify software programs to meet the needs of students with special needs.

C/H   Hannaford, A., & Taber, F. M. Microcomputer software for the handicapped development and evaluation. *Exceptional Children*, 1982, *49*(2), 137–142.
This article basically deals with the subject and problem of evaluation for use of educational microcomputer software for handicapped learners. The importance of consideration of educational compatibility, instructional design adequacy, and technical adequacy are stresses for those who develop or evaluate software specifically for this population.

C/H   Hasselbrine, T. S. Remediating spelling problems of learning handicapped students through the use of microcomputers. *Educational Technology*, 1982, *22*(4), 31–32.
This microcomputer program provides the student who had been unable to spell satisfactorily, regardless of the reason suspected, with individual spelling remediation using imitation and modeling techniques.

C/H   Helge, D. Technologies as rural special education problem solvers. *Exceptional Children*, January 1984, Vol. 50, No. 4, PS. 351–360.
This article addresses the availability of new technologies and their uses in educational supports application, management and staff development. Problems of new technology use in rural education are addressed, and successfully used models are described.

C/H   Hofmeister, A. M. Microcomputers in perspective. *Exceptional Children*, 1982, *49*(2), 115–121.
Although microcomputers will undoubtedly make a contribution to special education, educators face problems because of the poor quality of some of the available computer-assisted instruction software and the limited supply of hardware. Careful implementation of the strengths of computer technology is necessary.

C/H   Hofmeister, A. M. Technological Tools for Rural Special Education. *Exceptional Children*, January 1984, Vol. 50 No. 4, PS. 344–350.
This article addresses special education problems of the rural population, and the value of computer use in addressing some of these problems. The concept of universal excellence in education is presented with the advantage the new technologies offer in pushing toward this goal.

C/V   Hogan, R. On-line computerized career guidance. *Behavior Research Methods and Instrumentation*, 1981, *13*(4), 613–615.

The background rationale and development of an on-line computerized career guidance system are presented, with special emphasis on the relationship between the conceptual theory and the working design for the system.

C/H   Howe, J. Computers: A researcher's view. *Education: Toward Trends*, 1980, *7*(4), 17–21.

The researcher's view is presented on issues that relate to the use of computer technology aids in education of handicapped students, particularly computer use with autistic, dyslexic, and learning-disabled children. The processes of programming and of learning are presented, as well as the relationship between learning and communication. Word attack skills, important in communication, are effectively taught to handicapped children by computer-based systems. This article also presents the valuable use to handicapped students of computers in simulating a system.

C/H   Howe, J. A. Computers can teach where others fail. *Technological Horizons in Education*, 1981, *8*(1), 44–45.

The use of computers in teaching handicapped students cursive writing, in testing the effectiveness of teaching methods for handicapped students, and in simulating systems such as composing tunes and even generating sentences is presented in this article. These computer-based instructional programs expand learning opportunities for the handicapped and are thought to improve instructional strategies for more effective learning.

H/V   Humes, C. Career guidance for the handicapped: A comprehensive approach. *Vocational Guidance Quarterly*, 1982, *30*(4), 351–358.

The author addresses the laws affecting the handicapped, particularly Public Law 94-142, the Education for All Handicapped Children Act, in terms of vocational education and career development for this population. The laws are presented as effective in forcing awareness of conditions that must be changed, which will also lead to attitudinal change, with the understanding that the laws themselves do not automatically affect attitudes toward the handicapped.

C/H   Joiner, L. M. et al. Microcomputers: An available technology for special education. *Journal of Special Education Technology*, 1980, *3*(2), 37–47.

As the title indicates, this article describes the technology that was available at the time (note the publication date in 1980) for use with special education students. The basic microcomputer system and its capabilities and features as well as its problems are presented. Special education applications noted include computer-assisted instruction, prosthesis, testing, communication, and enhancing personal relations. Problems noted are availability of authoring languages, high-quality educational software, and computer safety.

H/V   Katz, A. H., & Martin, K. *A handbook of services for the handicapped*. Westport, Connecticut: Greenwood Press, 1982.

Chapter 4, entitled "Employment and Vocational Rehabilitation," presents a rationale for vocational rehabilitation, concepts of handicapping versus disabling conditions related to vocational demands, and a description of available programs. The Vocational Rehabilitation process, eligibility, services, and politics of the agency operation are also presented.

H/V   Kiem, R., Rak, C., & Fell, G. Career awareness for handicapped students. *The Education Digest*, 1983, *48*(5), 57–63.

The article presents and describes the Work Study and Special Needs Programs of the Cleveland Public Schools, which were established on the rationale that assisting handicapped students to become economically self-supporting prior to or upon graduation is necessary for self-growth and self-respect. The components of vocational evaluation and vocational adjustment are described.

H/V   Kokoska, C. J. Career development for exceptional individuals. *Teaching Exceptional Children*, 1983, *15*(4), 197–198.

This article discusses the need for coordination of career development services for the handicapped between the public school and vocational rehabilitation, with an emphasis on the broad concept of career as a totality of one's experience including paid and unpaid work, personal life-styles, and other social roles.

C/H   Lally, M. Computer-assisted instruction for the development of basic skills with intellectually handicapped school children. Canberra: Australian Education Research and Development Committee, 1981.

This is an individual report discussing the uses of computer-assisted instruction for the learning disabled in teaching handwriting, reading, and concept formation in mathematical problems, including the use of digitizer light pen and special display screen for the handwriting instruction. The reading instruction uses computer synthesized speech and a special input panel. An interactive color computer system is used for instruction in concept formation, and conservation of numbers and development of spatial concepts are addressed. An investigation into the effectiveness of the approach and the problems of practical application of educational technology research are described in this report, with an overview of CAI and its use in improving educational possibilities for the learning-disabled student.

H/V   Levitan, S. A., & Taggart, R. *Jobs for the disabled*. Baltimore: The Johns Hopkins University Press, 1977.
The author presents this study, which emphasizes the similarities, differences, and implications of vocational rehabilitation versus manpower programs, as a part of a more extensive review of vocational rehabilitation. It first encompasses employment, socioeconomics, changing labor market, and interrelationship of problems of disabled individuals, after which the vocational rehabilitation rationale and systems are presented as related to state/federal programs, aid for disabled veterans, and sheltered workshops for the severely disabled. The underlying issues of disability and rehabilitation are then investigated, including: 1) what constitutes disability and a need for rehabilitation; 2) public financial investment in rehabilitation programs for the disabled; 3) priorities for service among the kinds and levels of disability; 4) the adequacy of services offered; 5) economic considerations of the disabled; and 6) the roles of social insurance and welfare benefits. The final section of the book addresses the absence of and need for assessment of the efficacy of vocational rehabilitation programs and their contribution in serving the disabled.

H/V   MacArthur, C. A., Hagerty, G., & Taymans, J. Personnel preparation: A catalyst in career education for the handicapped. *Exceptional Education Quarterly*, 1982, *3*(3), 1–8.
In recognition of a greater need for career development and education for handicapped students, this article proposes cooperation and collaboration of private and public resources to improve and expand models of career and vocational education for the handicapped. The recommendations made include use of the current delivery of service and changes in those systems, and integrating new approaches that emphasize career education and development. Included as additions and changes to existing programs would be education specialists, the business community, financial support, and use of effective models.

C/H   Macleod, I., & Procter, P. A dynamic approach to teaching handwriting skills. *Visible Language*, 1979, *13*(1), 29–42.

The cases of three 13- and 14-year-old students who had previously been unable to learn to sign their names legibly and correctly are presented with the computer system that was used satisfactorily to teach them this skill. The system uses a graphic display screen and a hand-held "pen."

C/H   Marsh, M. Computer assisted instruction in reading. *Journal of Reading*, 1983, *26*(8), 697–701.

This article discusses early computer-assisted reading projects, reports the results of research studies, and suggests avenues for future curriculum development and research. Culturally disadvantaged children, the study suggests, would benefit from instruction on computers.

C/H   Mason, R. Reading a reading disorder. *Health*, 1982, *14*, 16.

BEAM (brain electrical activity mapping), which maps electrical activity in the brain and projects it onto a television screen, is enabling researchers to compare brain activity in both hemispheres and activity of experimental and control groups. This has allowed for an early diagnosis of dyslexia and for more information of what actually goes on in the brain of a dyslexic child. The procedure is also being used in an effort to determine the presence of unique electrical brain signatures in schizophrenia, epilepsy, and depression.

C/H   McDermott, P. A., & Watkins, M. W. Computerized vs. conventional remedial instruction for learning-disabled pupils. *The Journal of Special Education*, 1983, *17*(1), 80–88.

In this effort to assess the effectiveness of computerized remedial methods versus conventional ones with handicapped learners, 205 learning-disabled children in grades 1–6 were assigned either to a CAI treatment group in math or spelling or to a control group receiving conventional instruction. The posttest performance, pretest achievement, IQ, and time in remedial instruction were taken into account. Gains for the three groups were found to be essentially equivalent; also, popular achievement measures were thought to be insensitive to achievement gains in the learning disabled. Suggestions of needed future research include relating these results to duration of impairment, motivation levels, and learning styles, and care in selecting measures that are adequately sensitive to achievement gains in handicapped learners.

C/H   McKinnon, A. L. An effective and convenient approach to the inservice preparation of teachers of mainstreamed exceptional children. Paper presented at the Council for Exceptional Children Conference on the Exceptional Bilingual Child, New Orleans, Louisiana, February 1981.
The Mobile Instructional Classroom (MIC), a concept and program of computer-assisted instruction and audiovisual resources, is presented here as a tool to aid in education of the handicapped. It allows flexibility of instruction for off-campus students, and was found to be motivating both for the handicapped and for the classroom instructor.

C/H   Microcomputers for the Visually Handicapped. *Education of the Visually Handicapped*, Winter 1984, Vol. XV, No. 4 Pgs. 108–144 (entire edition).
This issue is devoted entirely to the topic, presenting four papers addressing research on multimedia access, evaluation of microcomputer access for this population, independence for the visually impaired through technology, and an evaluation of microcomputer instruction programs for the population.

H/V   Mori, A. A. Career education for the learning disabled: Where are we now? *Learning Disability Quarterly*, 1980, *3*(1), 91–101.
This overview of current career development theory and practice for the learning disabled includes emphasis on development of career and self-awareness, personal qualities and attitudes that affect career selection and performance, and skill development to meet requirements of entry-level positions.

C/H   Moyles, L., & Newell, J. Microcomputers in a postsecondary curriculum. *Academic Therapy*, 1982, *18*(2), 149–155.
Cabrillo College, a 2-year community college in Aptos, California, has developed a learning skills program that utilizes microcomputers to enhance their diagnostic and instructional programs offered to learning-disabled adults. Their program is described in this article.

H/V   Mulhall, J. F. The apprenticeship of the handicapped: An interactional analysis of the disruption and reconstitution of the social careers of physically disabled persons. Dissertation paper, The University of Connecticut, Storrs, 1981. (Order #8117605)
This study investigates the disability process and career reconstitution of 34 individuals identified as paraplegic, revealing three major variables that significantly affect their return to work or reconstitution of careers. These variables are: the

severity of the paraplegia, the age of the participant, and the time span between the beginning of the disability and any stage of the process of reconstituting one's career. It also identifies social handicaps resulting from the physical handicap, and proposes prevention and treatment strategies. There is an emphasis on the interaction of social and physical disability; 34 proposals for further research are suggested.

H/V   Muraski, J. A. Experience based career education for learning disabled adolescents. Dissertation paper, University of Southern California, Los Angeles, 1981.

Eighteen learning-disabled students were compared to 15 learning-disabled students in order to study the effects and benefits of an experiential career education program for this group of disabled youths. The factors defined as significantly affecting career development and adjustment to work included cognitive ability, academic achievement, daily living competencies, and career maturity. The experiential career program was found to significantly improve academic achievement and career maturity as well as severity of disability and motivation to participate in school. The program was not effective in addressing cognitive ability and daily living skills needs. The author concludes that learning-disabled individuals do have specific deficits that affect career development, some of which can be significantly improved by participation in an experienced-based career education program for the learning disabled.

C/V   Myers, R. A., Cairo, P. C., Turner, J. A., & Ganzberg, M. Cost-benefit analysis of the Officer Career Information and Planning System. U.S. Army Research Institute for the Behavioral and Social Sciences. August 1980.

This article addresses the efficacy of a computer-aided manpower management and career progression system, which has been developed to include a means of estimating costs and benefits of its implementation. The program is entitled Officer Career Information and Planning System (OCIPS), and is a computer-operated system described here in the light of the goals of the Officer Personnel Management System and the problems of the Army Military Personnel Center in pursuing these goals. A plan for an operational system, estimated costs, and a comparison of installation strategies and equipment alternatives are presented. The costs of this program are also compared to the costs of disseminating career information without computers.

C/H/V Office of Education (DHEW). Development and field test of a multi-purpose computerized vocational counseling program for providing placement, occupational and educational information to unemployed adults, handicapped persons and inmates in correctional institutions. Project Results, Final Report, Vol. 1 of 3. Washington, D.C., March 1979.

The purpose of the project was to develop a computerized vocational counseling program for use by unemployed/ underemployed adults, handicapped persons, and prison inmates. Vocational and counseling needs of the clients were assessed, an occupational information computer package was developed, and occupational information as well as employability skills were addressed through sound filmstrips. The program was tested in Tennessee with a population of unemployed or underemployed adults, handicapped persons, and prison inmates. Evaluation data indicated that the program was well received, and that it significantly increased the users' knowledge of the world of work.

C/V   Penn, P. D. Differential effects on vocationally-related behaviors of a computer-based career guidance system in conjunction with innovative career exploration strategies. Dissertation paper, June 1982. University of Minnesota, Minneapolis.

The question asked was whether or not computer-based career guidance systems affect vocational behaviors of non-high school graduates ages 16–24 when used with innovative exploration strategies. DISCOVER was used in each of the three experimental groups, alone in the first, with "life-style" filmstrips in the second, and with Psychsocial Visit Exploration (interview) in the third. The three conclusions noted are: 1) DISCOVER does affect certain vocational behaviors of this group; 2) for 22–24-year-olds DISCOVER is particularly effective in conjunction with Psychosocial Visit interview; and 3) vocational maturity may be independent of occupational preference.

H/V   Phelps, L. A., & Lutz, R. J. *Career exploration and preparation for the special needs learner.* Boston: Allyn and Bacon, 1977.

A team effort approach focuses on individual and unique needs of participants, services of which are designed to lead the handicapped individual through a program of occupational development culminating in the optimum competencies to aid the individual in functioning independently in an appropriate occupational role in society. The book is divided into two sections: The first addresses the cooperative roles and needs in career education and preparation of disabled students, and the second section presents the process of instructional programs and a systematic approach designed for development and management of these programs.

C/H   Reece, H. F. Computers, learning styles, and instructional materials—Are they related? *Academic Therapy*, 1982, *18*(2), 157–161.

With the apparent belief that computers used for delivery of instructional materials adapted for specific learning styles form a related and useful tool in education of the handicapped, the author describes a system that helps learning-disabled students and their teachers to select instructional materials most likely to be of benefit to them individually.

H/V   Robinshtein, S. Y. Work activity for the mentally ill. *Soviet Neurology and Psychiatry*, 1981, *14*(1–2), 65–81.

This article presents a review of the Russian literature as well as guidelines for vocational counseling of the mentally ill. No specific considerations are presented for those who receive specific skills education, and this seems to be the best approach. Complications arise, as reported, when a mentally ill person remains in regular school until seventh or eighth grade and has already encountered many failures, and this population is reported to be vocationally unstable. Skills required for a vocational counselor working with mentally ill patients are presented, and the populations among the mentally ill requiring special training are noted.

C/H   Rockwell, D. L. Application of task analysis of the design of CAI programs. *American Annals of the Deaf*, 1982, *127*(5), 585–590.

Computer-assisted instruction can be evaluated on the basis of whether or not the instruction achieves the objectives by a task analysis applied to the design of the program. Specifically in relation to programs for handicapped students, the task, accompanying decisions and steps, learning skill involved, and specific objectives are identified in conjunction with the results.

C/V   Sampson, J. P., & Pyle, K. R. Ethical issues involved with the use of computer-assisted counseling, testing, and guidance systems. *The Personnel and Guidance Journal*, 1983, *61*(5), 283–286.

Particularly relating to counseling in career and college centers, the author addresses the easy availability of use and data in terms of client use and confidentiality, stressing the need for counselor intervention where computer aids are available in these and other areas.

C/H/V   Sampson, P., Jr. Measurement forum—Computer-assisted testing and assessments: Current status and implications for the future. *Measurement and Evaluation in Guidance*, 1983, *15*(3), 293–299.

Among the potential benefits of computer-assisted testing and assessment are "assistance to individuals with visual, auditory, and physical limitations," requiring minimal staff assistance in the area of career assessment and interpretation. The article addresses the broad range of testing and assessment, noting the many potential benefits for all populations, including handicapped, such as positive client response, cost-effectiveness, adaptive testing, ancillary services and data, better use of staff time, time saved in administration and scoring, fewer errors related to test use, interpretive reports more valid and reliable, assistance for handicapped users, and opportunities for further research. Potential problems, including removal of the human factor, are addressed; potential benefits and problems provide material for implications for the future, including integrating human factors, ethical issues, reliability and validity regarding occupational alternatives, integration with existing services, exposure to the system by users, and continued development and research.

H/V   Sarkees, M. D., & Gill, D. Vocational education's role in the comprehensive delivery of services to handicapped individuals. *Career Development of Exceptional Individuals*, 1981, *4*, 89–95.

The role of the vocational education program, as presented in our public high schools, is reported and defended in this article. The six generally recognized program areas are described, followed by a discussion of the three delivery mechanisms of specific skills instruction, cooperative education instruction, and youth group affiliation. The place of vocational education within the comprehensive delivery of educational services is presented, describing the five vocational education delivery options of regular vocational education, adapted vocational education, special vocational education, individual vocational training, and prevocational evaluation services. Finally, responsibilities of vocational education are elaborated, with a final statement in support of the program when presented with basic understanding of its effective use.

C/H   Schiffman, G., et al. Personal computers for the learning
       disabled. *Journal of Learning Disabilities*, 1982, *15*(7),
       422–425.
Barriers to implementation of use of computers in the field of
special education, specifically the learning disabled, with
suggested solutions, are presented, as well as the usefulness of
computers in management of the individualized programs in
educating the learning disabled.

C/H   Semmel, M. I., et al. Microgames: An application of microcom-
       puters for training personnel who work with handicapped
       children. *Teacher Education and Special Education*,
       1981, *4*(3), 27–33.
Special education teachers can be trained in behavior management simulation by the program presented here, with the use of
microcomputers. The four software packages focus on the
behavior game, feedback, computer-assisted instruction, and
computer-guided implementation of behavior management.

H/V   Stodden, R. A., & Ianacone, R. N. Career/vocational assess-
       ment of the special needs individuals: A conceptual model.
       Exceptional Children, 1981, *May*, 600–608. Vol. 47.
Stodden and Ianacone present a conceptual model for the
career/vocational assessment of special needs individuals. After
a review of existing assessment procedures and a delineation of
10 conceptual considerations important to the development of
an assessment model, the authors present their model, which
consists of three components: readiness, assessment, and
application. Readiness includes awareness, exploration and
understanding of self, and general occupational cluster areas.
Assessment calls for an in-depth work assessment of specific
work-related and work skills. Application calls for interpretation, evaluation, and preparation of data for application. The
authors stress self-awareness, awareness of options, and ability
to make choices/decisions regarding a vocational future, as well
as involvement of significant others in a team approach.

C/H   Stowitschek, J. J. Applying programming principles to remedial
       handwriting practice. *Journal of Special Educational
       Technology*, 1978, *1*(1), 21–26.
Thirty-four learning-disabled primary school-aged children were
tested on the applicability of a computer program designed to
improve and speed the learning of handwriting skills of this
population. The program adapts conventional worksheets and
workbooks to this medium of instruction.

C/H   Tawney, J. W., & Cartwright, O. P. Teaching in a technology
            oriented society. *Teacher Education and Special Edu-
            cation*, 1981, *4*(3), 3–14.

This article, intended to increase the teacher's awareness of
revolutionary technical developments, presents a futures orientation, describes direction of major technical thrusts, and
describes specific communication and mobility products that
special education teachers should know about.

C/H   Thomas, M. A. Educating handicapped students via micro-
            computer/videodisc technology: A conversation with ron
            thorkildsen. *Education and Training of the mentally
            Retarded*, 1981, *16*(4), 264–269.

Ron Thorkildsen, Director of a research project on micro-
computer/videodisk and computer-assisted instruction for
handicapped individuals, discusses in this interview micro-
computer/videodisk technology future outlook in use for
education of handicapped students, as well as his own research
and development project in this field.

C/H   Thormann, M. J. Public school use of computers in special
            education. Dissertation paper, March 1983. University of
            Oregon, Eugene.

The study investigates computer use for special education in
Oregon public schools in the light of benefits and problems of
this computer usage. The computers were reported to be highly
motivating and to boost the special education student's self-
esteem. Teachers and administrators were interested in the
use.

C/H   Torgesen, J. K., & Young, K. A. Priorities for the use of
            microcomputers with learning disabled children. *Journal of
            Learning Disabilities*, 1983, *16*()4), 234–237.

This article proposes a set of priorities for the development and
use of computer resources with elementary-aged learning-
disabled children; contentions are that the priorities are different
for learning-disabled children than for children who learn
normally, and that computer applications among learning-
disabled adolescents will be different from those among
learning-disabled younger children. The two guiding principles
are the principle of uniqueness requiring computers be used in
ways that cannot be duplicated by less expensive means, and the
principle of educational necessity indicating that computer use
address the most critical needs first. The first priority suggested
is to provide practice activities for the development of efficiency
in reading individual words, in that maximum use could be made

of computer resources in the area of reading and word decoding, which causes the most important problems for learning-disabled children. Microcomputers offer the opportunity for repetitive individual word practice, which traditional instruction does not provide. Three aspects should be emphasized in the computer software: perceptual recognition speed, meanings of words, and speed of access to "semantic word knowledge." Limitations of the hardware are noted, with ways to program around the difficulties.

C/H   Vance, B., & Hayden, D. Use of microcomputers to manage assessment data. *Journal of Learning Disabilities*, 1982, *15*(8), 496–498.

A computerized special education management system, which is designed to provide an efficient and uncomplicated method of tracking data of educational and psychological evaluations, is described. It is used to manage assessment data for exceptional students.

H/V   Vandergoot, D., & Worrall, J. D. (Eds.). *Placement in rehabilitation—A career development perspective*. Austin: PRO-ED, 1979.

The concept of long-range career development for disabled people is the scope of this book, which consists of a beginning chapter by the editors that conceptualizes placement and career needs of disabled people and how vocational rehabilitation may more adequately address these needs, followed by 10 chapters written by experts in response to various aspects of rehabilitation. The first of these responses addresses the roles and functions of rehabilitation professionals and suggests changes. The second presents a suggested counseling approach based on a concept of how vocational development occurs. The third, directed to both counselors and administrators, advocates structured planning in career development including realistic evaluation. The fourth asserts the need for labor market information in career planning for the disabled. The fifth addresses the role and responsibility of job developers to be aware of the need for and identify new technologies in employment. The sixth stresses job analysis and its benefits for the disabled and the employer. The seventh, in conjunction with the sixth, addresses job restructuring and environmental modification for the disabled in career planning and services. The eighth response encourages consideration of life and career development after placement. The ninth describes the need for labor market information and tailored job training and preparation. The last response speaks to the important aspect of staff training and development for the rehabilitation worker.

C/H   Vensel, G. J. Changes in attitude of preservice special educators toward computers. *Teacher Education and Special Education*, 1981, *4*(3), 40–43.

A microcomputer system demonstration was presented to a group of 23 special education teachers who were, prior to their first teaching assignment, not favorable toward the use of computers in the classroom. The demonstration reports that there was a "large shift" in the attitudes of the teachers as result of the demonstration.

H/V   Walker, A. The handicapped school leaver and the transition to work. *British Journal of Guidance and Counseling*, 1980, *8*(2), 212–223.

The author presents a study of 500 18-year-olds in an effort to determine the difference between handicapped and nonhandicapped in their use of counseling services before leaving school and/or for employment counseling. Nonhandicapped students used counseling services twice as often as handicapped students both before leaving school and for later employment counseling. The author concludes that further development in counseling services for the handicapped is indicated.

C/H   Watkins, M., & Webb, C. Computer assisted instruction with learning disabled students. *Educational Computer*, 1981, *1*(3), 24–27.

An investigation of the effectiveness of computer-assisted instruction with learning-disabled students in an elementary school is presented, with the finding that this population was able to increase their mathematical skills by taking advantage of computer-based instruction.

C/H   Watson, P. G. Utilization of the computer with deaf learners. *Educational Technology*, 1978, *18*(4), 47–49.

The many operative and possible applications of computer use in education of the deaf and, to a lesser degree in this article, the handicapped, are presented. Communication needs served by computer use, particularly for the deaf, are also reviewed.

H/V   Wehman, P. Toward the employability of severely handicapped children and youth. *Teaching Exceptional Children*, 1983, *15*(4), 220–225.

Observations elicited from several job placement programs that were successful for mildly, moderately, and severely handicapped persons include: 1) vocational programs for the severely handicapped begin too late (between ages 14 and 16); and 2) employment and job placement do not receive heavy emphasis in most school-based vocational programs. These aspects contribute to the maintenance of high unemployment of handicapped individuals. Guidelines are presented for time commitment of vocational training activities for severely/profoundly handicapped students throughout the school years, a sample vocational task plan is presented, and the roles of related personnel are delineated.

C/H   Weir, A. The computer as a creative educational tool. *American Annals of the Deaf*, 1982, *127*(5), 690–692.

The use of the LOGO system in individualized instruction for handicapped students is presented. It is designed to serve a broad range of students, including those with various handicaps, and emphasizes the learning process as opposed to an emphasis on specific results.

C/H   Wexler, H. Rescuing trapped minds. *American Education*, 1980, *16*(6), 38.

This brief article presents the use of the computer system called LOGO in releasing the minds of severely handicapped and otherwise uncommunicative children. Any motor signal that the student is able to make is harnessed and translated, allowing the individual to communicate thoughts, answer questions, and issue commands.

H/V   Wilson, W. Facilitating the career attitude maturity of disabled college students through career awareness groups. Dissertation paper, North Texas State University, Denton, 1981. (Order #8128304)

This study was conducted to determine whether or not career awareness groups which use Guided Imagery and/or the California Occupational Preference System will affect career attitude maturity of disabled college students. Three experimental groups—one using Guided Imagery, one using the California Occupational Preference System, and one using both—were compared to the control group. Results showed that use of the California Occupational Preference System alone as well as in conjunction with Guided Imagery did increase career attitude maturity of this population, whereas the use of Guided Imagery alone did not show an increase.

The following two sections include: 1) names and addresses of periodicals reviewed for the bibliography including the 1983 editions reviewed individually; and 2) selected publications, conferences, and institutions devoted, in whole or part, to rehabilitation technology and engineering.

Periodicals

Academic Therapy
　　20 Commercial Boulevard, Novato, California 94947
Alberta Journal of Educational Research
　　Doyal Nelson, Editor, Faculty of Education, 845 Education South,
　　The University of Alberta, Edmonton, Canada T6G 2G5
American Annals of the Deaf
　　814 Thayer Avenue, Silver Spring, Maryland 20910
American Education
　　Superintendent of Documents, U.S. Government Printing Office,
　　Washington, D.C. 20402
American Educational Research Journal
　　American Educational Research Association, 1230 17th Street,
　　N.W., Washington, D.C. 20036
American Journal of Mental Deficiency
　　1719 Kalorama Road, N.W., Washington, D.C. 20009
American Psychologist
　　APA, 1400 North Uhle Street, Arlington, Virginia 22201
American School Board Journal
　　1055 Thomas Jefferson St., N.W., Washington, D.C. 20007
Association for Computer Machinery Journal
　　11 West 42nd Street, New York, New York 10036
British Journal of Educational Studies
　　Basil Blackwell (Publisher), 108 Cowley Road, Oxford, England
　　OX 41JF
BYTE
　　P.O. Box 328, Hancock, New Hampshire 03449
Computer World
　　Box 880, 375 Cochituate Road, Framingham, Massachusetts
　　01701
Computers and Education
　　Persamon Press, Inc., Maxwell House, Fairview Park, Elmsford,
　　New York 10523
Computers and People
　　Berkeley Enterprises, Inc., 815 Washington Street, Newtonville,
　　Massachusetts 02160

Contemporary Education
   M. Dale Baighman, Editor, Statesman Towers, Room 1005, Terre
   Haute, Indiana 47809
Continuum (Journal of the National University of Continuing Education Association)
   National University of Continuing Education Association, One
   Dupont Circle, Suite 360, Washington, D.C. 20036
Creative Computer
   P.O. Box 5214, Boulder, Colorado 80321
Curriculum Inquiry
   The Ontario Institute for Studies, 252 Bloor Street West, Toronto,
   Ontario, Canada M5S 1V6
Datamation
   875 Third Avenue, New York, New York 10022
Education
   Box 566, Chula Vista, California 92010
Education Digest
   Box 8623, Ann Arbor, Michigan 48107
Education and Urban Society
   Sage Publications, Inc., 275 South Beverly Drive, Beverly Hills,
   California 90212
Education of the Visually Handicapped
   Heldref Publications, 4000 Albemarle St N.W., Washington, D.C.
   20016
Educational Communication and Technology
   Association for Education Communications and Technology, Inc.,
   1126 Sixteenth Street, N.W., Washington, D.C. 20036
Educational Forum
   Kappa Delta Pi, P.O. Box A, West Lafayette, Indiana 47906
Educational Leadership
   Association for Supervision and Curriculum Development, 225
   North Washington Street, Alexandria, Virginia 22314
Educational Media International
   The Modino Press, Ltd., Keswick House, 3 Greenway, London N20
   8EE Great Britain
Educational Psychologist
   Thomas J. Shvell, Editor; Dept. of Counseling and Educational
   Psychology, 409 Christopher Baldy Hall, State University of New
   York at Buffalo, Buffalo, New York 14260
Educational Record
   One Dupont Circle, Washington, D.C. 20036
Educational Research Quarterly
   University of Southern California, Los Angeles, California 90007

Educational Studies
Robert R. Sherman, Managing Editor, College of Education, University of Florida, Gainesville, Florida 32611
Educational Technology
140 Sylvan Avenue, Englewood Cliffs, New Jersey 07632
Elementary School Journal
University of Chicago Press, Journals Division, P.O. Box 37005, Chicago, Illinois 60637
English Journal
National Council of Teachers of English, 1111 Henyon Road, Urbana, Illinois 61801
Exceptional Children
CEC, 1920 Association Drive, Reston, Virginia 22091
Harvard Educational Review
Longfellow Hall, 13 Appian Way, Cambridge, Massachusetts 02138
High School Journal
University of North Carolina Press, Box 2288, Chapel Hill, North Carolina 27514
History of Education
Publications Expediting, Inc., 200 Meecham Avenue, Elmont, New York 11003
IBM Journal of Research and Development
International Business Machines Corp., Armonk, New York 10504
Instructional Science
Journal Information Center, Elsevier Science Publishing Co., Inc., 52 Vanderbilt Avenue, New York, N.Y. 10017
Journal of Applied Rehabilitation Counseling
NRCA, 8136 Old Keene Mill Road, Suite A-307, Springfield, Virginia 22152
Journal of Career Education
College of Education, University of Missouri-Columbia, Columbia, Missouri 65211
Journal of Counseling Psychology
APA, 1400 North Uhle Street, Arlington, Virginia 22201
Journal of Educational Measurement
National Council on Measurement in Education, 1230 17th Street, N.W., Washington, D.C. 20036
Journal of Educational Psychology
APA, 1200 Seventeenth Street, Washington, D.C. 20036
Journal of Educational Research
4000 Albemarle Street, N.W., Washington, D.C. 20016

Journal of Educational Thought
Faculty of Education, The University of Calgary, 2500 University Drive, N.W., Calgary, Alberta, Canada 72N 1N4
Journal of Experimental Education
HELDREF Publications, 4000 Albemarle Street, N.W., Washington, D.C. 20016
Journal of Higher Education
Ohio State University Press, 2070 Neil Avenue, Columbus, Ohio 43210
Journal of Learning Disabilities
11 East Adams Street, Suite 1209, Chicago, Illinois 60611
Journal of Reading
International Reading Association, 800 Barksdale Road, P.O. Box 8139, Newark, Delaware 19714
Journal of Rehabilitation
National Rehabilitation Association, 633 South Washington Street, Alexandria, Virginia 22314
Journal of Research and Development in Education
G3 Aderhold Building, University of Georgia, Athens, Georgia 30602
Journal of Special Education
111 Fifth Avenue, New York, New York 10003
Language Arts
National Council of Teachers of English, 1111 Kenyon Road, Urbana, Illinois 61801
Mathematics Teacher
1906 Assocation Drive, Reston, Virginia 23091
Measurement and Evaluation in Guidance
American Association for Counseling and Development; 5999 Stevenson Drive, Alexandria, Virginia 22304
Peabody Journal of Education
George Peabody College for Teachers of Vanderbilt University, Nashville, Tennessee
Personal Computing
P.O. Box 2942, Boulder, Colorado 80322
Personnel and Guidance Journal
American Association for Counseling and Development, 5999 Stevenson Drive, Alexandria, Virginia 22304
Pointer—For Educators and Parents of Exceptional Children
Helen Dwight Reid Educational Foundation, 4000 Albemarle Street, N.W., Washington, D.C. 20016
Programmed Learning and Educational Technology

Logan Page, Ltd., 120 Pentonville Road, London N1 9JN
Psychology in the Schools
4 Conant Square, Brandon, Vermont 05733
Reading Improvement
Project Innovation, Box 566, Chula Vista, California 92010
Reading Research Quarterly
International Reading Association, 800 Barksdale Road, P.O. Box 8139, Newark, Delaware 19711
Reading Teacher
International Reading Association, 800 Barksdale Road, P.O. Box 8139, Newark, Delaware 19711
Reading World
College Reading Assocation, 3340 South Danbury Avenue, Springfield, Missouri 65807
Rehabilitation Counseling Bulletin
ARCA, American Association for Counseling and Development, 5999 Stevenson Drive, Alexandria, Virginia 22304
Remedial and Special Education (Formerly *Journal for Special Educators)*
PRO-ED, 5341 Industrial Oaks Blvd., Austin, Texas 78735
Research in Higher Education
Agathon Press, Inc., 15 East 26th Street, New York, New York 10010
Review of Educational Research
American Education Research Association, 1230 17th Street, N.W., Washington, D.C. 20036
School Science and Mathematics
Gary G. Bitter, Editor, Arizona State University, 203 Payne Hall, Tempe, Arizona 85287
Science and Children
National Science Teachers Association, 1742 Connecticut Avenue, N.W., Washington, D.C. 20009
Scientific American
415 Madison Avenue, New York, New York 10017
Sociology of Education
American Sociological Association, 1722 N Street, N.W., Washington, D.C. 20036
Spoken English—Ideas and Developments
ESB (International) Ltd., 32, Roe Lane, Southport, Merseyside PR9 9EA
Teaching Exceptional Children
CEC, 1920 Association Drive, Reston, Virginia 22091

Urban Education
429 Christopher Baldy Hall, State University of New York, Buffalo, New York 14260
Volta Review (for Deaf Concerns)
Alexander Graham Bell Association for the Deaf, 3417 Volta Place, N.W., Washington, D.C. 20007
Work and Occupations
Sage Publications, Inc., 275 South Beverly Drive, Beverly Hills, California 90212

Selected Publications

For the following selected publications in rehabilitation technology and engineering, with annotations, we have relied heavily on James R. O'Reagan's paper "Rehabilitation Technology in the 1980's," as noted in our preface.

Able Data   The Catholic University of America, 4407 Eighth Street, N.W., Washington, D.C. 20017
Provides computer search bibliography on hardware and software computer technology aids for the disabled.
Accent on Living   Cheever Publishing, Inc., P.O. Box 700, Gillum Road and High Drive, Bloomington, Illinois 61701.
Published quarterly, this magazine addresses independent living technology aids for the disabled.
Annual Reports   Rehabilitation and other centers provide, on request, the most currently available information regarding center operations and technology.
Bulletin of Prosthetics Research   Rehabilitation Engineering Research and Development Service, Department of Medicine and Surgery, Veteran's Administration, Washington, D.C. 20402
This quarterly provides current bibliography of rehabilitation engineering publications, current literature abstracts, and product information of assistive devices.
Bulletins on Science and Technology for the Handicapped   American Association for the Advancement of Science. Office of Opportunities in Science, 1515 Massachusetts Avenue, N.W., Washington, D.C. 20005
Listing of current workshops and meetings.
Handicapped Funding Directory   Eckstein, B. J., Research Grant Studies, P.O. Box 357, Oceanside, New York 11572

This directory lists foundations, grant agencies, and associations granting funds for handicapped programs and services.

Johns Hopkins APL Technical Digest Johns Hopkins University Applied Physics Laboratory, Johns Hopkins Road, Laurel, Maryland 20707
Volume 3, Number 3, July–September 1982, special issue "Personal Computer Aids for the Handicapped Issue." This issue contains 14 theme articles addressing the Johns Hopkins national search; aids for the hearing impaired and other communication devices; computer technology for brain-injured, motor-handicapped, and visually impaired individuals; and product availability. Other articles address urban transportation, use of ultrasonics, and the European Solar Energy Conference.

Proceedings of the Annual Conference on Rehabilitation Engineering Rehabilitation Engineering Society of North America, Suite 210, 4405 East-West Highway, Bethesda, Maryland 20814
Recording of the latest engineering developments in the field of rehabilitation.

Research Directory of the Rehabilitation Research and Training Centers Department of Health, and Human Services, National Institute of Handicapped Research (NIHR), Special Centers Program, Mary Switzer Building, Washington, D.C. 20201
The directory includes abstracts of individual NIHR Projects.

Resource Guide to Habilitative Techniques and Aids Codman, Elizabeth, Job Development Laboratory, George Washington University, I Street, N.W., Room 420, Washington, D.C. 20037
Resource of information and equipment available to cerebral-palsied adults.

Institutional Resources

Again, for the institutional resources selected that provide rehabilitation services with the use of technology and engineering, we have relied heavily on Mr. O'Reagan's "Rehabilitation Technology in the 1980's" paper.

Assistive Devices Center (ADC) California State University, 600 J Street, Sacramento, California 95819
Generalized assessment services with an emphasis on communication aids.

George Washington University Job Development Laboratory 2300 I Street, N.W., Room 420, Washington, D.C. 20037
Job reengineering for severely disabled persons.

New York University Rehabilitation Engineering Center Institute of Rehabilitation Medicine, 400 East 34th Street, New York, New York 10016
Concerned primarily with persons with high level spinal cord injury, this center conducts projects to determine suitable use of commercial electronic assistive devices for rehabilitation of this population.

Northwestern University Rehabilitation Engineering Program Room 1441, 345 East Superior Street, Chicago, Illinois 60611
Conducts projects to determine improved and appropriate technical support systems for severely disabled persons.

Smith-Kettlewell Institute for Visual Sciences—Rehabilitation Engineering Center 2232 Webster Street, San Francisco, California 94115
Research and evaluation of sensory aids for blind and visually impaired persons.

Texas Rehabilitation Commission—Project IMPART 118 East Riverside Drive, Austin, Texas 78704
This is a public resource service that searches for individualized solutions to rehabilitation engineering problems.

Tufts Biomedical Engineering Center 171 Harrison Avenue, Boston, Massachusetts 02111
Development of communication aids for nonvocal individuals.

University of Michigan Rehabilitation Engineering Center Department of Mechanical Engineering, W. E. Lay Automotive Laboratories, Ann Arbor, Michigan 48109
Assistive driving devices and systems.

University of Virginia Rehabilitation Engineering Center P.O. Box 3368, University Station, Charlottesville, Virginia 22903
Research, development and evaluation of technical aids and systems with special emphasis on mobility.

Veterans Administration Prosthetics Center (VAPC) 252 Seventh Avenue, New York, N.Y. 10001
Development, evaluation, and service delivery of technical aids with emphasis on spinal cord injury, mobility, and transportation.

Wichita Cerebral Palsy Research Foundation of Kansas Rehabilitation Engineering Center P.O. Box 8217, Wichita, Kansas 67208
Vocational aspects of rehabilitation.

Woodrow Wilson Rehabilitation Center Fishersville, Virginia 22939
Rehabilitation of severely disabled individuals, with special emphasis on vocational aspects of rehabilitation.

Index